The history they don't want you to know …

DEMOCRATIC COMA

Dr. Virgil Brannon

Book Publishers Network
P.O. Box 2256
Bothell • WA • 98041
PH • 425-483-3040
www.bookpublishersnetwork.com

10 9 8 7 6 5 4 3 2 1

Printed in the United States of America

ISBN 978-1-937454-45-6
LCCN 2012942434

Editor: Julie Scandora
Cover designer: Laura Zugzda
Typographer: Leigh Faulkner

Dedicated to the future of my sons, Justice and Austin.

In memory of Dr. Martin Luther King Jr.

CONTENTS

ACKNOWLEDGMENTS

Above all, I thank God for giving me wisdom, knowledge, and the courage to write *Democratic Coma.*

I thank my wife, Tiffany, for her support. And I thank my boys for working with me. I love you guys. Both of you have played an important role in my life and in helping me shape the *Democratic Coma.*

I thank Erica U. for sending me two of the most patient and caring individuals a writer could have, Miss Dona Curtis-Thomas and Mrs. Judy Jenkins. Miss Dona, thank you for helping me format and organize my written thoughts. Your aggressive encouragement, tolerance, and high spirit in the truth I will never forget. Judy, thank you for your editing talent, your kindness, and your loving spirit in being there when I needed you. I will always remember your willingness to help me while in pain, and your contribution will be that legacy you always talked about. You are a fighter, and I will forever fight for you.

Finally, Julie Scandora, thank you for sharing your brilliancy, your knowledge, and your final touch in editing my book. Your promptness and patience mean a lot to me. Sheryn Hara, thank you for seeing the vision and executing the plan of action with no hesitation. You are everything I wished for in taking on this project.

THE COMA

I

Awakening: The True Beginning

Before now, politics had never been my strength, but common sense has always been my friend; whenever I have stopped to observe or research a matter, I usually discover the truth. In 2008, I stopped my own activities to research history to understand why we as Black Americans were failing most. I found the truth within our leaders and the Democratic Party that we so loyally serve. This answer was a shock; it was as if I had awakened from a coma. I wondered to myself, "What was I thinking? How had I missed it?" It was so obvious to me now. This awareness started on a Halloween night while observing the custom of trick or treat and the scare tactics that mirrored the Halloween celebration. It was then that I awoke to find myself afraid, feeling trapped by the Democratic Party, as if I were caught in a Halloween haunted house with no one to rescue me. To have missed this, I must have been in a coma, a coma that had kept me from seeing that a haunted house is a symbol of the Democratic Party.

The Democratic Party has been using fear tactics to keep us spooked and controlled. That fear has destroyed our confidence and sense of self, which ultimately destroys families, communities, and racial harmony. This kind of fear tactic causes persons who believe the message to pass the blame of failure on to anyone or anything other than themselves; at the same time it causes more and more dependence upon the treats that the Democrats promise to hand out to the faithful. That same tactic is being used to demonize the Republican Party; if you are a Republican, you are somehow evil and racist. However, in my research, I discovered who really is.

You see, all my life, I was a Democrat, and so was my mother, my sister, and my brother. As for my father, he never voted because he never trusted politicians. But for me, I trusted the Democrats, and I voted. I trusted that they would properly educate our youth, I trusted that they would create opportunities for any man to succeed in America, I trusted that they would find a solution to solve the poverty of the less fortunate, and I trusted that they would tell us the truth and not lie to us. I was a loyal Democrat who voted faithfully with no questions asked because I saw many black faces that looked like me, quoting Dr. Martin Luther King Jr. I voted straight Democrat because I believed it was the party for Black Americans and for me and my family. I was convinced that they had my best interests at heart, never suspecting that their only interest was in getting my vote.

As November 4, 2008, was approaching, I watched America gradually set aside its tradition of having White American male candidates for president take a chance on a Black American male. Not only did we see the potential of having the first Black American for president, but we also saw the possibility of having a woman as a president. It seemed as if America grew overnight into a better place. Americans as a whole could boldly turn to their children and say with confidence, "America has changed. This ends racism. You can be anything you want to be in America, including the president of the United States of America." There are over forty-two million Black Americans living in the United States; not all of them voted for Mr. Obama, yet he still won. Sixty-seven million Americans voted for Mr. Obama. The numbers suggest that a large percentage of Hillary Clinton's eighteen million supporters voted for Mr. Obama, too. There were also Republicans and Independents that crossed party lines to join the Democrats in support of "Hope and Change." The night of November 4 was historical; the "Dream" of Dr. King seemed to be fulfilled. Not only did we have a Black American president, but also there were more Black Americans who paid attention to politics and came out to vote than ever before.

Now when I look back and witness the economy at the brink of a worse depression, see unemployment continuing to rise, home ownership continuing to disappear, and oil prices going up at an alarming rate, I think, what is going on with the Democratic Party. I turned on the radio and heard conservatives criticizing the president's actions as anti-American. I then turned on the liberal radio stations and heard many reasons why we cannot criticize the president. This puzzled me, but I continued to think that the main reason was that he was Black. The same thing was found on television stations, both on the left and right; all crowning the president as a new Black god that realized the "Dream." Then I reevaluated the "Dream" speech to see if it had been finally fulfilled. I continued to pay attention and listen and saw that most of the Black leaders were not satisfied with the presidency of Obama. I started to look deep into this matter to find that almost half of those same Black leaders were, in fact, destroying that very "Dream" with their own racism and hatred and that the "Dream" would never be realized in the climate created by these politicians and activist leaders. Each problem that the country faced was blamed on White Americans and the Republican Party. The "Dream" did not stand a chance. This worried me, but I continued to ponder the matter.

There are two written documents that are dear to me: the Holy Bible and the Constitution and its Amendments. Not only are these two documents precious to me, but I also trust them. In my search for the truth, I wanted to see whether the Democratic Party's actions would be accepted by our Founding Fathers as seen in their writings related to the drafting of the Constitution. I found that the Founding Fathers stood on their beliefs and values that every man should have the *"unalienable Rights, ... Life, Liberty and the pursuit of Happiness."* This statement led me to really think and to wonder why a slave owner would later have a change of heart to free slaves that were profitable to him or her. The finding was quite stunning and consistent with their beliefs. In a debate on freeing slaves during the late 1700s, the Northerner told the Southerner, "How can we call this a free country when we allow one man to own another?" Northerners had less use for slaves because their farms were too small to support feeding and housing laborers all year, the cooler weather made a shorter growing season, which also kept earnings low to support year-round workers, and industrial factories were starting up, replacing the farming economy. As a result, the Northerners started helping the slaves escape from the South. As for the Southerners, they had plantations, very large farms for producing many crops, like cotton and tobacco, which required slaves.[1] They were not looking to stop slavery; their only concern was to find ways to keep it going.

I then turned to the Bible, the book on which the Constitution was built, to rethink and compare the message. I concluded that we all have the God-given right to succeed. America's history lined up with the Bible: every man should be free to live his life in serving his own god according to his own conscience. However, it has become very clear that, under today's leadership, we are not going down the right path for what this country was founded on. I found that the Democratic Party does not want us to succeed; their policies are against basic Biblical values and teachings. I found that the Democratic Party was "faking faith"; they had broken almost every one of the Ten Commandments. First: *You shall have no other God before me*; the Democrats worship power over the welfare of the people, as well as call themselves the alternative to God.[2] Second: *You shall not make any idols*; the Democrats call themselves leaders and impose themselves on the poor and the needy to be worshipped. Third: *You shall not take the name of the Lord in vain*; the Democrats have  taken the Lord's name in vain by removing it and prayer from many public schools and almost all government buildings, including military cemeteries.[3, 4] If that is not enough, they have also used Jesus's name in vain in an effort to raise taxes on hard-working people.[5] Fourth: *Honor your father and mother*; the Democrats have created programs to separate and remove the father from his home, which fosters a loss of the children's respect for their parent. Fifth: *You shall not murder*; the Democrats' policies and programs have destroyed Black families all across the nation by manufacturing poverty. Sixth: *You shall not steal*; the Democrats have taken away Blacks' freedom, stolen taxpayers' money, and laundered it through the failed and dummy companies of their shadow friends and campaign donors. This made me think. Is the Democratic Party, the party of sin? The president's actions surely look anti-American. His policies seem as if they are destroying the basis on which this country was founded. This country was founded on the teachings of the Bible. This list goes on and on for how the Democrats work.[6]

After picking up the Bible, old history books, and science books, I became even more driven to learn about America and her purpose as a nation and what today's America has become. I continued to think! I cannot be the only one that can research and find answers to the entire Black American problem without any help from a so-called leader. History has proven our leaders and the Democratic Party have failed us. It is only a matter of time before all of us will accept it because voting, praying, marching, and a sometimes well-spoken speech have gotten us nowhere but broke because being stuck in poverty just won't do.

2

Deficiency: A Father's Failure

I supported the president; I even campaigned for him with my two sons holding signs with his name on them and passed out flyers that I created and printed with my own money. We stood on corners with a bullhorn, spreading the words, "Go vote." I sent campaign contributions in an effort to secure his presidency, and I stood outside of my polling station directing voters where to park.

I marched with Al Sharpton in Jena, Louisiana, in support of the six young boys who were in a fight with some other young white boys. I marched on the United States Justice Center in Washington to let my voice be heard for the unjust laws that hinder true justice as defined under the Fourteenth Amendment.

Because I already was working with young people, I started a youth program to encourage, inspire, and teach our children about finding and using their God-given abilities through entrepreneurship, science, mathematics, and determination. I offered a summer camp to teach the children about the Constitution, but no one showed up. I went to several community recreation centers to get help in expanding my vision, but all of them prefer the children just to play. I called out to a local television judge to see if she could speak to the children for one minute on a small camcorder, but her assistant told me it would be twenty thousand dollars or find another way to raise the money, an amount that I did not have. I did all the things that I could do to help the children, the president, and Al Sharpton succeed. After all the hoopla had died down, I had time to sit and think about the Black American plight in America. I found that the problem was, just simply, us.

We Black Americans gave the president 92 percent of our vote, one of which was mine. We helped in creating the problem. I had failed to see that this was just a game of manipulation in which the president had related to Blacks in a way that got our votes. His speeches were not intended to inspire Black men to take care of their families or to encourage them to start businesses but, rather, to promote the Democratic Party's agenda in expanding poverty, racism, and dependency—modern slavery. This agenda's success has resulted in the separation of families, leaving Black men with no hope and no chance of getting ahead because most men are lost without their families and homes. Still, today, many of us cannot figure out why we are at the bottom of every class and the lowest in all statistics when it comes to education. In essence, why are we failing in life, failing to help ourselves with God's help, failing to love and praise each other's efforts or do the right thing as God commanded us to do? We have created false gods.

You see, I wanted the president to succeed, but when there is a problem and we are told by so-called leaders on radio stations not to criticize him or hold him accountable for what he says or does, this essentially helps the president to fail. In other words, by not holding him accountable, what we are really doing is assisting him in failing; and when he fails, the whole Black American race suffers with the possibility of another forty more years of setbacks and failures. One of the biggest mistakes ever is that too many of us place too great an importance on having a Black American president, so much so, that we neglect to hold him accountable for his performance as a president. We judge him based on how he looks. Whatever happened to judging a man by the "content of his character"? This is the direct opposite of Dr. M. L. King's non-racial agenda. We did not research to learn who Obama was nor what his beliefs, policies, and values were; we just voted for him because of the color of his skin, thinking that he would automatically know our problems and care. It seems that he did not understand what his country was all about or who his base of voters was or what his focus should be. Those who voted him into office could never have imagined that he had not walked a mile in their shoes. Our guaranteed vote of 92 percent did not help us; it just hindered us.

We as Black Americans have never petitioned Mr. Obama about any of our issues, such as poverty, police brutality, home ownership, or job loss. Today, we still have not presented our agenda to the president. The only agenda that has been met are those of the likes of Al Sharpton, and to date, he may be one of the few Black Americans that has actually prospered from Mr. Obama's presidency. As I questioned the matter, I was convinced I had been tricked into the Democratic Coma, blinded by the treat that is skin color and false hope for change. Never again will I just vote for color; instead, I will inspect the character of the person. I embarrassed myself in front of my two boys, crying on that election night and screaming at the top of my lungs, calling out another man's name. I did this outside the voting poll in front of numerous people, too. I went against every personal rule and value to ensure that President Obama was elected.

During the 2008 primary, all I had on my mind was, "He is Black. He knows our struggle." Little did we know he had never stood in our shoes or lived in our communities. He was sent to the Trinity Church to learn the Black culture and to build a voting base. He has never been profiled against, he has never tried to grow a small business and live from paycheck to paycheck, and he has never had a loan or a grant denied. What was I thinking of by allowing myself to be used by these people? What was worse, it was done in front of my boys. Never in a lifetime could I have imagined that I would allow someone to trick me into this trap of dependency with my eyes wide open. This trap was set just to get votes from us, never to help me or other hard-workers and other hard-working entrepreneurs around the country maintain a successful business or even to be able to hire more people. There was nothing in this for the benefit of the voter.

My loyalty to the Democratic Party has helped to create a deficiency in our economy far beyond my imagination; but as a Black man, all I could see was the color of this man's skin and the possibility of having the first Black president. I failed my family by not recognizing the truth. I let color blind my judgment when it came to picking the candidate to oversee my future as well as the future of my children. Unfortunately, I let the color of a single man's skin speak to me instead of seeking the truth about the man before I gave away my vote so freely. My heart is deeply saddened because I failed my family and, most of all, my country because Obama is just one piece of the game plan of the Democratic Party's game of trick or treat.

This party's game plan is to wait, hoping that we never rise to find the truth about the value of education. Most important, they hope that we never come to grips with the truth and awaken from the Democratic Coma, the Coma that has kept us from knowing that the Democrats were the ones who opposed freedom, the Emancipation Proclamation and the Thirteenth Amendment. They also opposed the Fourteenth Amendment and the Fifteenth Amendment. The Democrats fought against the Freeman Bureau Act in 1865, which was to assist former slaves in their transition to freedom with food, clothing, housing, education, and job contracts after the Civil War.[1] This is the only time assistance should have been given because there were absolutely no other alternatives during those times.

As I continued to look deeply into the Democratic Party and the problems that hinder Black Americas to become just Americans, I was awakened to other facts. It was simple. This party created hate to divide us. These were all the things that many of us took for granted in learning or just were not paying attention to in school. This new knowledge completely confirmed that I was in the Coma, the Coma of not knowing that the Civil Rights Act of 1866 was opposed by the Democrats. I did not know that they were against the Reconstruction Act in 1867, the Enforcement Act of 1870 that protected Blacks after the Civil War, the Ku Klux Klan Act of 1871, and the Civil Rights Acts of 1866 and 1875.[2, 3, 4]

I was in the Coma of not knowing that the Democrats controlled the House of Representatives for forty years straight between the years of 1954 and 1995.[5] For thirty-four of those years, they also controlled the Senate, writing and passing laws hindering "The Dream" and the Black American families from evolving.[6] In fact, those same exact years contained the struggle of the Civil Rights Movement.[7] Think about it. They opposed the case of *Brown v. the Board of Education* in 1954.[8] They rallied against the case of Emmett Till in 1955, calling themselves the "Uptown Clan."[9] They opposed the case of the Little Rock Nine in 1957.[10] They also opposed the case involving Rosa Parks. They were in charge during the Watts Riot in 1965 with Democratic Governor Pat Brown.[11] The Democrats were in charge in the 1963 bombing by Ku Klux Klan member Bobby Frank Cherry of the 16th Street Baptist Church in Birmingham, Alabama, that killed four young girls.[12] Then there was the murder of Medgar Evers by Byron De La Beckwith, a member of the White Knights of the Ku Klux Klan later in that same year.[13] Just about in every significant event concerning Blacks that you can find between those years, the Democrats' hands were in it. This made me think that Dr. King could not have been a Democrat; this party was going against everything that Dr. King Jr. and others were fighting for during that era. The Democratic Party was also against the Civil Rights Acts of 1954 and 1968, and they were against the United States Commission on Civil Rights, which Republican Dwight Eisenhower signed into law.[14] The commission's responsibility was to investigate and report anything that threatened one's civil rights.[15] All of this proves that the Democratic Party has deliberately covered up history while we were asleep in the Coma.

Some things still caused me confusion due to this Democratic Coma so I looked at the laws that were being passed right after slavery ended. I found out that the Democratic Party passed discriminatory Black Codes and Jim Crow laws against Blacks.[16] In the case of *Plessy v. Ferguson*, Homer Plessy, a light-skinned man who was one-eighth African and seventh-eighths White, tested the laws by purchasing a ticket to ride a train car from New Orleans to east Louisiana and attempting to sit in a "for Whites only" seat. Plessy was later arrested and convicted for not sitting in an appropriate section "for Blacks only." In that case, it was Justice John Harlan Marshall, a Republican who was nominated and appointed by Republican President Rutherford B. Hayes to the Supreme Court, that disagreed with the case in a seven to one vote. Harlan argued against the majority and wrote, "In the eyes of the law in this country, there is no superior, or dominant, ruling class of citizens; the Constitution is color-blind, and does not tolerate classes among citizens."[17]

The Democrats supported and passed the Missouri Compromise to protect slavery in 1820, in other words, to keep it going.[18] They supported and passed the Kansas Nebraska Act to expand slavery by allowing the new settlers to decide if they would allow slavery or not. They supported the Dred Scott Decision, they opposed educating Blacks, and they fought for lynching laws that terrorized Blacks in the South.[19, 20] Their last known kleagle in the Ku Klux Klan was Democrat Senator Robert Byrd of West Virginia, who died in 2010 during the second year of the Obama Administration. Byrd was famous for holding a fourteen-hour filibuster in an effort to keep the Civil Rights Act of 1964 from passing.[21]

The Democrats passed the Repeal Act of 1894 that overturned civil rights laws enacted by the Republican Party; because of the Republican support for Blacks, the Democrats said they would rather vote for a "yellow dog" than vote for a Republican.[22] When Democrat President Woodrow Wilson took office in 1913, he reenacted the segregation laws throughout the federal government. Not only was President Wilson against integration, but also Democrat President Franklin D. Roosevelt appointed Senator Hugo Black, a lifelong member of the Ku Klux Klan, to the Supreme Court in Alabama, and in 1944, he chose Harry Truman to be his vice president who had joined the Ku Klux Klan in Kansas City back in 1922.[23, 24]

The Coma continued. As if all this was not enough, Democrat President Franklin Roosevelt fought against Republican efforts to pass a federal law against lynching and for Blacks being in the armed forces during the 1964 Civil Rights Movement. Also, during that time, Democrat Governor Orval Faubus tried to prevent the desegregation of the Little Rock public schools, but it was denied by Republican President Dwight Eisenhower. During Dr. King's protest in Birmingham, Alabama, it was the Democrats he was fighting and protesting against, including the Democrat Public Safety Commissioner, Eugene "Bull" Connor, who unleashed dogs and turned fire hoses on Black civil rights demonstrators.[25] Democrat Georgia Governor Lester Maddox refused to serve Blacks in his restaurant and prevented them by waving his famous axe at them. Democrat Governor George Wallace declared that the schools in his district would be forever segregated.

Many of us may think that Democratic Senator John F. Kennedy was for Black Americans, but he voted against the 1957 Civil Rights Act along with Democrat Senator Strom Thurmond, who is on record for giving the longest filibuster ever, twenty-four hours and eighteen minutes straight.[26, 27] Kennedy also opposed Dr. King's 1963 march on Washington, and his younger brother Robert Kennedy, who was the Attorney General for Lyndon Johnson, had Dr. King wiretapped and investigated by the FBI. There are many of you that might feel as though Democrat President Bill Clinton was the first Black president, but he did his internship with his mentor, US Senator J. William Fulbright, an

Arkansas Democrat and a supporter of racial segregation. How else could Bill Clinton be so smooth at fitting in? His mentor Senator Fulbright and one hundred other members of Congress (ninety-nine of whom were Democrats) signed the Southern Manifesto that opposed integration in all public places.[28, 29] This was passed after the Supreme Court's 1954 *Brown v. Board of Education* decision. Fulbright also joined with the Dixiecrats in the filibuster to prevent the Civil Rights Acts of 1957 and 1964 from being passed.[30, 31, 32]

So like many of you, by now I wanted to know who really killed Dr. King Jr. We know James Earl Ray did, but what were his beliefs, what did he value, and who did he look up to? What kind of man would do such a thing? After days of researching this matter, I found that in 1967 Ray had a huge interest in helping Alabama's Democrat Governor George Wallace run for president because of their like-minded hatred of Black Americans and their commitment to preserving segregation.[33] Ray spent a large amount of time volunteering at Wallace's North Hollywood headquarters in Los Angeles, California.[34]

Moreover, in his 1958 run for governor, Wallace lost the primary election to Democrat John Patterson who, ironically, had the support of the Ku Klux Klan and most Black Americans.[35, 36] Wallace turned up his hatred for Black Americans and stated in a conversation with his finance director, Seymore Trammell, "I was out-niggered, and I will never be out-niggered again."[37] Later, after Wallace's loss, a supporter asked why he started using racist messages. Wallace replied, "You know, I tried to talk about good roads and good schools, all these things that have been part of my career, and nobody listened. And then I began talking about niggers, and they stomped the floor."

In 1963 at his inaugural address for his first term as governor, he affirmed his stand against Black Americans in stating:

> It is very appropriate that from this cradle of the Confederacy, this very heart of the great Anglo-Saxon Southland, that today we sound the drum for freedom as have our generations of forebears before us time and again down through history. Let us rise to the call for freedom-loving blood that is in us and send our answer to the tyranny that clanks its chains upon the South. In the name of the greatest people that have ever trod this earth, I draw the line in the dust and toss the gauntlet before the feet of tyranny, and I say segregation now, segregation tomorrow, segregation forever.[38, 39]

Remember, this is the man whom James Earl Ray admired and volunteered for. Not long after Wallace's run for president had failed on November 2, 1967, six months later on April 4, 1968, Ray assassinated Dr. King. James Earl Ray was a Democrat who thought his Democratic mentor had good ideas for stopping Black Americans, but when Wallace lost the primary election, Ray took it upon himself to plot and kill the Blacks' leader, Dr. King Jr. (I later discovered that Dr. King was a Republican.)[40] All of these events point to a deficiency that has hindered Black Americans and placed us in this Democratic Coma that prevents us from learning the truth about history and the people who have not helped us.

My common sense and research show that the Democratic Party's agenda has failed a race of people and brainwashed them by preventing them from finding the real truth about the Party and the direction in which they are trying to take this country. This party has created a deficiency within the Black-American communities by preaching bondage, slavery, and dependency; and for others, they have created an uncomfortable racial environment. They neglect to tell Blacks that they are free and just need to learn about

American life and laws. Due to this, a great number of Blacks are deficient, dependent, and incapable of taking charge of their circumstances. This deficiency has discouraged us from researching the things that we do not understand. In addition, this deficiency has resulted in an upside-down way of thinking. Many of us think that we have somehow advanced in life; instead, we have regressed, causing us to continue to fail rather than grow and prosper. Too many of us Blacks think with our emotions and refuse to think with sound, unbiased, fact-based reason.

I watch many Blacks in America love everything and everyone but themselves. There are many that cannot understand why the Black race is still at the top of every statistic in having the worst schools, worst communities, and worst self-confidence and achievement, as well as the highest rate of unemployment. The crime rate among Blacks in America is very high, especially Black-on-Black crime. How can we hurt each other? I see how we have stopped competing for anything or with anyone to achieve something really positive and good. In fact, the only time we are ever competing is playing in a youth ball game or looking for jobs. The Democratic Party teaches us to fear ourselves by making us think that we were born to struggle and born to be in poverty for the rest of our lives. They have taught us to lean on them for help in exchange for our vote. We do not need them to hold us up or hold our hand to cross the street; we can get to the other side by ourselves if they will just get out of our way.

America is on the brink of changing, and there is just not enough time left before all of us will fall deeper into this deficiency because of our ignorance. We must recognize the truth that many of us have deliberately voted for the wrong party with the wrong leadership because we refuse to be rational. I allowed myself to be tricked into not seeing the underlying truth that poverty and dependency have been manufactured by the Democratic Party. They offer a mother food stamps and other government assistance in exchange for destroying her family by diminishing the role and purpose of a father in the home. As a matter of fact, in order for the mother to receive assistance from the government, in most instances, the father cannot be a part of the household. Afterward, they offer her child support, another program designed to make sure the father does not reappear. When the father does not pay, in most states, his driver's license will be suspended, resulting in minimizing his visitation with his children.

As long as the father is not in the home, he cannot raise his family. He will not be available and ready to instill good values, skills, and strength into his children because he is not there to make the day-to-day corrections. When you strip a father of his responsibilities, you are, in fact, stripping his family away and, in many instances, forcing the mother to compromise her dignity. Too many mothers end up depending on the government for help because they cannot visualize a better alternative. The government's alternative is just enough to keep breath in the body but not enough to remove one's self from poverty and all that it comes with. At this point, the government's monthly payments to the mother are essentially keeping the father out of the home and forcing the mother to become another victim of the Democratic Party's Democratic Coma/Trick Trap. In all fairness, the fathers who have never tried to be the man of the house ignore their families' plight. In fact, they are not prepared to help and, in most cases, do not know how to seek and accept help. These families, in most instances, are damned if they do and damned if they do not without any help.

Even when I broke down the meaning of the word *democrat*, it revealed this Democratic experiment against Black Americans. The word-part *demo* means a sample, an example or demonstration of something that has been tested or needs to be tested, and anything that needs testing is a part of an experiment. The word-part *crat* is a member of a dominant group or groups; if you research the word *dominant*, you get commanding, controlling, or prevailing over all others.

Under this system or experiment, we are not the one in charge or in control; we are the guinea pig. We are a sample, an experiment, just another subject for a powerful group. We are provided with assistance to make us dependent on those in power, which will eventually result in our total loss of personal power. We have given up our choice whether to choose for government assistance or not. The choice is made: either we vote for the Democratic Party, or we lose our government help. Understand that we have been tricked and fooled into believing that this group of dominant people's agenda is not to help us but to instill fear in us in place of our faith in ourselves and our God. My intention is to keep this truth before my eyes, lest I forget.

EXAMINING THE COMA

3

The Trap: Isolated from the Truth

A trap is a device or tactic intended to catch an intruder or an enemy.

—Wikipedia

For among my people are found wicked men: they lay wait, as he that setteth snares; they set a trap, they catch men.

—Jeremiah 5:26

When the doors of the unemployment office are open but no one is willing to hire, when the cost of living constantly rises, and when the banks are skeptical about giving loans to new owners, what is it called? A trap! When a large percentage of Black American eighth graders read below fifth-grade level, many Black American students fail every year to pass placement tests, and there has not been any solution offered for the problems, what is it called? A trap! If you are given free clothing, free food, free shelter, and free health care, what is it called? Slavery! So when all of these things are happening to you and you are told all of your life that you do not have a purpose, and they make it appear as though you are not free and that a whole race of people is against you, what is it called? The Democratic Coma!

The Democrats lied to us. They isolated us from the facts, leaving no room for the truth. We have been trapped in this party for too long; we have become brain dead to our own history. Many do not want to know the truth because then they will have no more excuses not to research for the truth and find their way home. The Democrats know the problem, but it is not part of their plan to correct it. Their plan is to keep us trapped in ignorance and from the knowledge that could save us.

We are trapped in fear, fear that lives on because we lack knowledge. And the cycle goes on and on. I know this truth may be hard for many of you to accept. So if you do not trust me, trust in yourself by researching and coming to your own conclusion. The only conclusion that I can come to is that, in order for Americans to rise, the Democratic Party must fall. We have been trapped by their selfishness and greed. We must recognize falsehoods in ourselves and in our leaders. They have purposely set traps to misguide many of us, and now we are victims of our fears.

The Democratic Party's traps are everywhere. There is a trap on every corner purposely designed to keep us "dumbed down." The trap of the liquor store cages us up in our communities. Throughout the years, this has affected our thinking and caused us to celebrate everyone else's successes except our own. False leaders do not want us to leave. Even the communities in which many of us live are traps. Some people call these communities "hoods." In these hoods, these poor communities, there are many stores designed to keep a poor man under the influence and confused—X-rated magazines to keep our minds perverted, cigars and cigarettes to shorten our lives, beer to make us raise hell, and whatever else we need to keep us content as victims of our own confusion. All are within an arm's reach of the store counters where we live. The trap of the Democrats has served its purpose; it has many of us sitting around looking lazy, some drugged-up, and others just watching mind-numbing television in a daze, while they play doctor with our lives.

How can we celebrate hope and change when many of us will not leave the party because we are too afraid to let go? I bet that next year, while the music is playing and their mouths are lying, we'll go cold turkey with the same tune and depend on them all over again. While we sat around celebrating Sasha's and Malia's lives in the White House, thirty thousand young mothers were trapped, sitting idle, waiting to be added to a waiting list for Section 8 housing to get some kind of shelter over them and their children's heads in East Point, Georgia.[1] There must be solutions put in place to stop this from happening.

The Generational Trap

I continued to research for more answers to the problems I found in the broken educational system that is failing so many of our youth. I found out that SACS, the Southern Association of Colleges and Schools, is an organization formed in 1895 to accredit over thirteen thousand public and private schools from preschool to college in the Southern part of the United States: Alabama, Georgia, Louisiana, Mississippi, Florida, North Carolina, South Carolina, Virginia, Kentucky, Tennessee, Texas, and later, Missouri.[2] Notice that all of these states were slave states and of the Confederacy that passed Jim Crow laws and where the KKK terrorized Blacks.[3] The question is, can this organization provide an objective evaluation of Black children or is this just another trap?

Are we trapping our children on the plantation of the poorly performing Southern schools run by Democrats with too many students per teacher, too few and too old books, and little opportunity for the children to learn about Jesus Christ? Many will say, "It starts at home," but if the knowledge is not there, to whom should the mother turn? Should she look for a false leader who has his or her own agenda? If the seed is not planted for growth, then to whom should a parent turn to get a harvest?

This educational system was designed to create permanent laborers, not entrepreneurs. I look at The No Child Left Behind Act, an educational program proposed to Bush in 2001 by the 107th US Congress for his approval, led at the time by the Senate president, Democrat Al Gore, Senate president pro tem Robert Byrd, and Dixiecrat founder Strom

Thurmond, all three of whom had some type of history fighting against the Civil Rights Act.[4] Why would we trust these gentlemen with our future if they did so poorly with our past? NCLB was a program that was designed to fund state schools, based on their achievement. Over the years, the program became a failure because of its strict requirements to test the children with no way to evaluate the teachers' performances. This program became a trap, setting the children back by two or three grade levels in reading, science, and mathematics. By the time a student graduates from high school, a large percentage of the children can barely read at a sixth-grade level. However, the solution will come if we can minimize our cultural obsession with beauty, appearance, popularity, and wealth and maximize our children's education so that they will have a first-rate chance to become middle class or better.

In Atlanta, Georgia, there was a cheating scandal in which almost two hundred teachers were investigated for cheating on the Criterion-Referenced Competency Tests (CRCT), a test that measures how well the students' skills and knowledge increase during a school year.[5] These teachers were caught erasing the answers and writing in correct answers so it would appear that more students had passed. As I thought about it, I realized that all these teachers are liberal instructors. Their aim is never to provide proper education but, rather, to mold loyal citizens who will belong to unions and vote Democrat. As a result, we have not advanced as a whole, and we certainly have not grown as Americans.

In a *20/20* special called "Stupid in America," John Stossel showed why public schools continue to fail in spite of having more government funding and union involvement. They were contrasted with thriving charter schools that are flourishing in all categories with less government assistance, no tenure for teachers, and almost no union at all. When the teachers do not produce, they are fired. The results are quite amazing; the students do better in charter schools. In this report, Stossel interviewed Nathan Saunders, president of the teachers union in Washington, DC. Saunders told Stossel, "Our test scores are not what we choose to focus on; we choose to focus on teaching children." Stossel replied, "But how do you know if they are learning anything if you don't test them to compare?" Saunders said, "I know my children are learning when I look in their eyes."[6] Saunders falsely thinks he is psychic, but obviously, he cannot see where he is guiding his students.

There was an article in 1996 in which technology guru Steve Jobs openly stated the total opposite of Saunders. Job said:

> The main problem with the educational policies and socio-political factors involved is that technology can't solve all these problems. I used to think that technology could help education. I've probably spearheaded giving away more computer equipment to schools than anybody else on the planet. But I've had to come to the inevitable conclusion that the problem is not one that technology can hope to solve. What's wrong with education cannot be fixed with technology. No amount of technology will make a dent. It's a political problem. The problems are sociopolitical. The problems are unions. You plot the growth of the NEA [National Education Association] and the dropping of SAT scores, and they're inversely proportional. The problems are unions in the schools. The problem is bureaucracy. [7]

Now here we are almost sixteen years later, and not one of our so-called leaders has investigated this technology genius's statement for truth. Something must be really wrong with this picture.

Look at it this way. In 2008, the unions gave the Obama campaign $206.7 million to be elected, and now for his re-election, they are planning to spend about $400 million.[8, 9] Our children do not stand a chance when the teachers' unions are buying the election to keep their jobs. How can the future be promising for students if failing teachers are protected by the union's political interests?

Debbie Squires, the Associate Director of the Michigan Elementary and Middle School Principals Association, was going back and forth with a member of the Michigan legislature. Squires stated, "Parents don't know what's best for their child."[10] Now, just because she is an educator does not mean she knows how to educate, especially when she presumes to know what is best for someone else's child. If this is so, then tell me why a large percentage of our children have been failing for years?

This puzzled me. So I did some research on the US Department of Education. I found that they have not educated anyone except to teach them how to be socialists and communists. One would think, based on the title, that they are educating people. The department was specifically formed, per their website, to "establish policy for, administer and coordinate most federal assistance to education, collect data on US schools, and to enforce federal educational laws regarding privacy and civil rights." In 2006, the Department of Education's discretionary budget was fifty-six billion dollars, and 50 percent went to them for administrating and 8 percent went back into the schools. As of 2012, they will receive sixty-nine billion dollars in discretionary budget, while the children continue to fail. This department's policies have failed. How much data and how many years does it take to understand there is a problem with education? This department was to provide over 150 educational programs and employ seventeen thousand people on an annual budget of $14.2 billion; however, it does nothing to educate our children. Since the passing of the Department of

Education Organization Act on October 17, 1979, by the 96th US Congress, a Democrat-controlled House, Senate, and president, this bill has been a failure from the start.[11] At the signing of the bill, Democrat President Jimmy Carter stated, "Our nation's educational system is the best in the world."[12] If that was so before signing the bill, why make any changes? Based on this alone, we can do without this department. How can the average child expect to receive a fair shot at a good education when the system appears to be a trap from the very start?

During the seventeenth century when public school was first established, most children were taught by ministers, but in today's society, many of our teachers have some type of disconnect with God. The main goal was to teach the children how to read so they could understand the Bible to connect with God and build a foundation of real principles and values. The Democrats have diminished our children's opportunities to grow in their relationships with God and, by so doing, contributed to their demise. A life without God creates a sense of emptiness and loss. Then the problem really starts to fester when we try to fill the place where God belongs with material things or people. This robbing of faith came about through the misrepresentation of a piece of a document that is reverenced and loved. This is one of the things that make this lie so effective.

All people consider the US Constitution to be a holy relic and thus should not be questioned. Some people take this sense of awe to the extreme; they refuse to read and research the document for themselves. The concept of "separation of church and state" has been given a new meaning that was not intended by the Founding Fathers of this nation. As a matter of fact, the Founding Fathers did about everything to ensure the very opposite of what is now promoted as "separation of church and state."

I proceeded to look into the matter more until the answer became clearer to me. On March 22, 1966, Republican

US House of Representative Everett Dirksen created and proposed the legislation to have prayer in the public school system. The Democrats, who controlled both houses, turned down this piece of legislation that year and every subsequent year it came up for a vote. Up until this point, many believed that Democratic President Lyndon Johnson was the author of the legislation, but history has provided the truth. Even Republican President Ronald Reagan took a stand on the matter with submitting his own amendment to allow school prayer in 1982, but it was also voted down. He stated, "We seek a constitutional amendment to permit voluntary school prayer. God should never have been expelled from America's classrooms in the first place." In 1985, the Republicans presented Reagan's plan again, but it failed again. In 1987, the proposal was passed for Senator Joe Biden to reconsider, but he refused to listen or even discuss it, so it never became law.[13] When you remove God from schools, you will have fighting and disruption, but if you place his name, his rules, and his love in a place with four corners, you'll get progress.

Compared to the rest of the world, America used to be at the top in science, but now, according to the 2009 PISA (Programme for International Student Assessment) worldwide evaluation report, we rank twenty-third compared with Shanghai-China at first.[14] In math, America ranks thirty-fourth, according to an evaluation by OECD (Organisation for Economic Co-operation and Development) from 2003 to 2006 with Indonesia in first place.[15] However, no matter how we measure the outcome, I'm willing to bet Debbie Squires is probably a member of a failing teacher's union.

Now, the Democrats want to control what the children eat by passing the Health Hungry-Free Children Act of 2010. On February 15, 2012, there was a story about a four-year-old that brought a lunch to school, and an inspector from the North Carolina Department of Health and Human Services took her turkey sandwich away and replaced it with breaded chicken nuggets.[16, 17] The inspector said it did not meet USDA's guidelines, but I bet if they had gone outside, they probably would have caught the inspector eating it. How can the government know what is best for the children if they cannot distinguish what is healthier, fried or cold cuts? Next time, they should spend more time hiring someone that is qualified to know the difference before telling a child her mother does not know what is best for her.

In the coming years, you will see more traps targeting our children, setting them up for more failure, igniting them into some type of uprising or violence in the streets. The Democrats' plan is to get our children to create riots, rebel against their parents, and attack innocent people on the streets. One of the so-called Democratic Party trappers of this agenda is Van Jones, a man that I like to call "Vampire Jones" or "Vamp," a man who is a self-avowed communist and anti-American, who likes to brainwash our youth by turning them against their country and parents. He has worked in the White House, the "Laboratory," working on policy until people found out he was a communist. He was quietly transferred during a weekend when reporters were not around to question his departure.

Since his transfer, he goes around to different schools, talking to children on how "not to listen to old people." Vamp has been caught telling children, "Don't listen to your parents; you are smarter than they are."[18] How outrageous for someone to go around implanting such an ignorant agenda in someone else's child and for the schools to invite him. They have used marketing to make us think that it is okay for our children to be taught in classrooms of thirty-five to forty students per teacher and then graduate them unprepared for college and uninspired to go. The children in public schools have been set up to fail, receiving the worst education ever under the Democrats. The party has planned this carefully, and every year we keep voting them back into office for the same failing treatment. As long as you do not challenge them, it will not get any better. Since the late eighties, Bill Cosby has been the only Black to promote positive images of other Blacks on television successfully with his sitcoms, *The Cosby Show* and *A Different World*, inspiring Blacks and other youth to go to college to do more with their lives. His shows have been a wonderful relief in contrast with other awful programs for our children to watch. In Atlanta, there is a director that creates characters showing a grandfather talking down to his grandchildren and demeaning the mother who is on drugs in front of the children. Now we have *Flava of Love*, *The Kardashians*, *Real Housewives*, and so many other reality shows that display no decent values for raising our children; instead these reality shows promote disrespect, sex, drugs, and everything unethical.

Before the 2008 election, the Black leaders were so critical of every president before President Obama. Now, not only do they continue to use us to help them gain more power, wealth, and prestige, but they also manipulate us to protect the reputation of the first Black president. They would rather scheme against us than present our demands to him or to hold him accountable for our futures and our children's futures. Every child in America's grade school system needs the best opportunity for a good education, with fewer students per classroom to learn better and to receive more attention from a caring teacher with creative skills, who is willing to take a struggling child and bring him or her up to standards by the end of the school year—for this would show a teacher's true ability.

All students who choose to go to college in pursuit of a science or math degree should receive a reduction in tuition because they are most apt to think of new innovations to help our economy and quality of life. In 2008, students were promised that they would receive five thousand dollars from the government, but where is it?[19] I hope that the policies of this president will not set this country and the Black population back, based on our blind trust and loyalty to him. For the last three years, this president has shown more concern for the Hispanic, the gay, and the Muslim communities than for any other community. Because many of us are not paying attention to politics, we have allowed others to make decisions for us. They have realized that there is profit in fear, so they have started businesses and campaigns to promote anything that they think can convert into fear and stir up trouble between groups.

No one is willing to talk about the long-term consequences of depending on food stamps and unemployment checks. They give us just enough information to make fools out of us. It should be a crime for our so-called leaders to withhold information from us and then tell lies to mislead us so they can make money for themselves. Their actions clearly show that they would rather help illegals and others instead of helping us. They would rather choose which group they will help instead of helping Americans as a whole. We cannot sit around and continue to say, "Give him a chance." We are at the bottom of the barrel; we do not have any more chances left. If we give him a chance on something that we know is not right and the president signs off on the bill, it becomes almost impossible to undo. It takes the other party's having a majority and enough time to repeal the law. By the time the bill is repealed, we can be even worse off economically, making the recovery last longer. This could be the worst mistake ever.

Making of the Chief Trapper

The president, the chief trapper, has trapped himself in George Soros's snare of power because he took funding from him. Has he made a deal with the devil, and can he repay his debt to avoid a disastrous end? When Obama was running for the Senate seat in 2006, the Brain introduced him to some of his elite friends to get their financial backing to run for president.[20] Soros has a bad reputation. He is known in

Thailand for "sucking the blood out of people." Soros is one of the richest men in the world, a billionaire from Budapest, Hungary, who has made most of his money bankrupting other countries by betting against their currencies—countries like Russia, Georgia, Hungary, Malaysia, and England.[21] As a fourteen-year-old boy, he worked to confiscate property from other Jews and lead them off to their death, which he claims was the best time of his life.[22] He owns the fifth largest hedge fund in the world, worth an estimated twenty-seven billion dollars. He has been caught on tape stating that his major focus is on America.[23] Soros has influenced President Obama's pushing socialism on us. This is where our country is going if we do not hold our president accountable. If we do not act now, we cannot complain when someone else becomes president who has an agenda that is not good for us or with whom we just disagree because of our ignorance of not evaluating and researching the candidate. The answer is simple; no matter who is president or even running for office, we must hold his or her feet to the fire so we can become more than just voters, but responsible voters.

History has proven that socialism does not work. More is gained in a capitalistic society than any other kind because the economic system provides incentives for the individual. Anybody can start a business today that provides a product or service that others want. You can make as much money as you want, depending on your interest and motivation. Many of us may not be ready to accept this fact, but this president has trapped all of us, White to Black; some are aware of what we face as Americans, but some of us have no clue that we are trapped. We find every excuse to blame anybody or anything but ourselves for voting, as I did, for the wrong person. How long will we continue to stand still and do nothing while others continue to take advantage of us? Every one of us has to take full responsibility for our actions, our time, and our efforts.

If you are waiting for someone to save you, no one is your savior but God. If every man who has left his family takes responsibility, returns home, and becomes the man that he is supposed to be, then our families and communities will flourish with strength and prosperity. We have spent too much time listening to false leaders and prophets telling us to "go vote," as though it is the secret code of the Black community that means "vote Democratic." How long will you sit around and continue to follow someone that has done nothing for you or who has not produced any results? There is no reason why we should be afraid of progressing; Black Americans have spent over four hundred years since the Atlantic Slave Trade, trapped in the same mess, oppressed, and deceived by false prophecy. Now, forty-eight years after being trapped in the Lyndon Johnson era, many of us have been waiting for a new leadership, but they are not coming. In case you have forgotten, Gandhi, King, Malcolm, Hosea, Washington, Jefferson, Lincoln—you name it—are all dead. Are you?

There is no reason for anyone not to pursue an education and/or his dreams. We all need education and training to develop ourselves, our gifts, and our visions to create a better future for us, our children, and this country we call America. There is no reason why a young man would want to wear his pants hanging down off his tail because this shows no positive sign of progress or growth; it just lowers his value and reflects badly on his family and his children. There is no reason for committing a crime because the consequences rob time away from the children and family and jeopardize the time a man could spend in discovering and using his talents and gifts. There is no reason to sell anything illegal because there are too many legal opportunities that are available for you and me to prosper from. There is no acceptable reason why a grown man should want to use his intelligence to deceive or manipulate a child for personal use for sex, money, fame, or power. There is no need for you to keep allowing leaders, politicians, family members, and even the president to manipulate you into getting what they want when you receive nothing respectable in return but slavery to the government.

These so-called Black leaders and their organizations should be helping these men find solutions for rebuilding their families after the government has taken their manhood away. These organizations are not providing them any assistance in obtaining visitation rights to see their children, they are not providing assistance for them to reestablish their lives back in the work force after being incarcerated, and they have offered nothing toward resolving poverty, racism, poor education, separation of families, or dependency. Saying nothing is equivalent to doing nothing. These men do not need these organizations to show up after the problems occur; they need them to help prevent the problems before they happen. If they are going to be leaders, they had better start being leaders. For years, these false leaders have been acting like most medical physicians by treating the symptoms without curing the underlying problem. The answer is pretty simple: stop writing prescriptions and start writing policies that can help these men rebuild their families and, in turn, make America a better place for all of us to live. If you say you are a leader, lead and present some solutions for these men's lives. This is a cultural deficiency that has been hindering the growth of Black American men. These organizations have done nothing since the death of Dr. King, with the exception of Hosea Williams's Feed the Homeless Foundation, which continues to feed thousands of people, Whites and Blacks, three to four times a year faithfully. So I ask you, are these leaders helping you or hindering you? If I did not know any better, I would think this Democratic agenda is an experiment on Black Americans to see how long we will voluntarily remain in this Coma.

In 1932, under the Democratic President Theodore Roosevelt, there was a forty-year study that was almost the same type of deadly experiment being administered as this Coma. In the Tuskegee Syphilis Experiment, the US Health Service conducted a study on Blacks in Tuskegee, Alabama, in which hundreds of Black men were secretly and purposely injected with the syphilis virus.[24] "The study would include four hundred Black men with syphilis and two hundred Black men that were non-contagious as a control group."[25] They called it a Syphilis Control Demonstration Program, which was conducted in six different locations: Macon County, Alabama; Scott County, Mississippi; Tipton County, Tennessee; Glynn County, Georgia; Pitt County, North Carolina; and Albemarle County, Virginia.[26] Again, the same states of the Confederacy, the KKK, and the Jim Crow laws. The men in this study thought they were getting free meals and free health care, but in reality, they were getting free meals and burials.[27] "The men were treated for syphilis with no treatment." You get it! These men were injected with syphilis, and then the researchers pretended as if they were treating them.[28] The same thing as the Democratic Coma—the Democrats are still pretending to help Black Americans and other minority groups, but all they are doing is making them more dependent. In other words, they are treating them for dependency and poverty with no real solution, just more entitlements. This is a TRAP ...

An Associated Press reporter, Jean Heller, on July 25, 1972, wrote, "The study was conducted to determine from autopsies what the disease does to the human body." Those men were guinea pigs for this study and tricked out of their health and lives by this disease. Once again, during this forty-year study, the Democrats controlled the House of Representative and Senate with the exception of two years, 1947–1949. It seems to me now that the Democrats cannot stop their madness; they continue to push something bigger and worse than the Tuskegee Experiment—the Democratic Coma. We have been injected with dependency from this party, and we have not found our way out.

Since 2008, we have been told not to do anything for ourselves but sit and wait for unemployment benefits, wait to have our children cared for, and wait to put our children in a better home and school. They have injected dependency into our minds to wait for them to help feed our children. They have injected this disease of poverty, lies, and abnormal teaching. This is nothing more than a Democratic doctrine and a Democratic philosophy used inside the Democratic Coma to experiment on Black Americans in order to accumulate more Democratic votes. The poorer you get, the richer they become—ask Al Sharpton.

Whatever we think we do not have is caused by believing that we cannot have it. We have been fed wrong ideas and wrong attitudes toward our lives. When the mind processes no data, it is because we have not given it the opportunity to input data, consider the information, and in so doing, expand its capabilities beyond our wildest beliefs. Our brains require information to expand. Every time we take in information, it is stored in our mind until the brain sends signals to retrieve it. However, when there is nothing there, our brain gives no response; and when there is no response, anger or fear is the result. This has trapped us in fear of ourselves because we choose not to understand the game that is being played on us. This is like playing football all your life and later deciding to take a paying job as a soccer coach; it will never work. Life and learning do not come easily; they always come with a price. Working to get paid is part of life's challenges, but you need training before you are ready for most jobs. For the rest of our lives, all of us will be a part of someone's trap if we are not alert. There is always someone waiting to prey upon our weaknesses and to test our faith. The purpose of a trap is to scheme to gain power over another individual who seems to be unaware. Do not get caught without tools to help you escape, or better yet, just do not get caught in the trap at all. Feed your mind with whatever gives you freedom and fulfillment.

I know that some of you may have forgotten that there are many who have successfully escaped the trap by taking action. A brave woman named Harriet Tubman escaped the trap; she led hundreds of slaves to freedom. A young man named Marcus Garvey escaped the trap; he started his own organization, the UNIA (Universal Negro Improvement Association), to help other Black Americans and a newspaper called *Negro World* that attracted millions of followers by promoting racial pride. A young lady named Oprah Winfrey escaped the trap; she became the first Black American billionaire and the richest Black American woman of the twentieth century as a talk-show host, actress, producer, and philanthropist. As of today, her business in on the verge of collapsing because she supported the president. A young man named Dr. Martin Luther King Jr. escaped the trap and changed a world of people from all walks of life. There have been many other wonderful Americans, such as George Washington, Abraham Lincoln, Dwight Eisenhower, and Ronald Reagan, that I will never forget because they have all contributed to our lives in a positive way.

The best way to deal with trappers is to be aware of them, know who they are, and prepare yourself to see through them from the inside out, but always be ready to face them mentally. A mental fight requires intelligence and patience, but it is always effective because no one believes that you have the courage and capability. They believe that you cannot make it without someone holding your hand, but you can.

4

The Indoctrination: The Making of a Patient

Behold, I will bring it health and cure; I will cure them and will reveal to them the abundance of peace and truth.

—Jeremiah 33:6

The Democratic Party is like a hospice; once you are in, the chances of leaving alive are small. The care that is provided is not inspired to get the patient well but to keep him comfortable until he dies. This party draws in people that have endured some kind of spiritual negligence or who have suffered some type of personal loss, emergency, or trauma. They house people in substandard housing and conditions that offer no hope. Like any medical facility, it functions with physicians who provide drugs to ease the dying and patients who give in to dying without fighting. The party is the facility that creates drug-like agendas and programs to make the patient addicted to his ignorance in the Democratic Coma. The patient is the voter that supports and votes for the doctors' agendas and programs in exchange for freebies, the "treats." When you study history, you will find that for every time you have endured a setback in your life, it was either from some type of Democratic doctrine, mythology, or someone who has manipulated or crippled your mind and advancement. These physicians are members of the party that has consistently destroyed Americans, enslaved them, and kept them from progressing in this country. They try to demolish your confidence, your responsibilities, your values, and your beliefs in God.

We are their patient transformed into their voter. They know that we are less likely to believe in ourselves while living in poverty and difficult environments. They know the lack of hope makes us most likely to have setbacks and most likely to have endured some type of medical problem in the past. Now, most of these physicians are members of the Democratic Party. They are often called elected officials or politicians or community activist leaders, which I sometimes call post-civil rights leaders. They can be anyone who wants to gain power over someone for self-profit after the Civil Rights Movement. Ask yourself one thing: why would these leaders join a party that has a history of opposing those same civil rights they say they are fighting for? To most politicians, you are only the means to their end. It is important to understand that it is not in the party's interest to teach you about your history. Their agenda is to create programs, movies, music, and jokes to keep us laughing so we will be too distracted, confused, weak, and dumbed down to pay attention to the real issues. For example, there are more rich Democrats than there are rich Republicans, but they won't tell you that; they will do everything in their power to keep that piece of information from you. Remember this is not about you; it is about their power over you.

Think about it: a politician walks in, making a yearly salary of about one hundred thousand dollars, and when he or she leaves politics after a few years, walks out with millions. Where did that sudden wealth come from? Did the politicians use their position while in office to negotiate their own business deals? No wonder it is difficult for the average politician to negotiate effectively for the people who put him or her in office. Instead of looking out for the voters, it is easier to tax the rich and distribute the money back to their donors. These politicians are too busy making their own deals to work for the benefit of the voters.

They sit back and wait for us to complain about a problem, they watch to see how we respond to the problem, and they look for allergic reactions or other side effects before prescribing themselves as the solution to our problems. False leaders do not want young mothers to cancel their food stamps or bring the father back into the home to do his job because then they could not buy her vote; instead, they would have to earn it. They do not want the father to pay the rent or the mortgage; they want him gone so they can manipulate the mother, showering her with expensive poverty and a dozen of dependency, just to remind her on "who's the daddy." You see, what we must understand is that as long as they keep offering her safe and secure poverty; she'll never leave because if they decrease the dependency dosage, it may cause her to depend all over again.

They want us to pick the wrong companions so we will have the wrong lives. They want young females to have babies out of wedlock so their lives can be unstable and chaotic; they want them to become dependent on social programs early in life, and they want the men to lead criminal lives so they can forever be in the system or on the run. They want us to be consumers forever instead of taking charge of our own lives and becoming owners and employers providing the products and services. They have no concern for what we do right; they just want us to vote left for Democrats to keep the "Solid South," a historical, ongoing movement. It is obvious they do not care! They do not care if the youth wear their pants sagging below their hips; this just helps them to identify their victims, the ones they think will most likely fail as fathers, be racially profiled, and become suspects in committed crimes. They need us to have problems so they can offer themselves as the prescription. The Democratic policy is to keep us down and disabled by telling us that we are weak and helpless. We are not weak; most of us are just uninformed. We are free; however, a part of freedom is the responsibility to think for one's self. So if the Democratic Party is the party for poor people and being poor means the lack of opportunity, then why should we claim a party that lacks providing it? The main part of life is growth and prosperity. At what point do we grow and prosper?

These Democratic physicians have us begging for more morphine, more entitlements to numb our disappointment. We are trapped in their agenda, and we continue to confuse ourselves about who we are. They have us quick to accept verbal traps of insult, like "nigger" and "bitch." Why would anyone want to be called names that mean "lacking in intelligence" and "a female who is sexually promiscuous or a dog," claiming to use them as forms of endearment or love? I would rather you hate me than love me if it mean you must belittle me in the same breath. Did we become what the South said we were, or have we become what we were once called? We cannot allow this trap to continue to play out in any neighborhood, White or Black.

I was in a grocery store in November 2010, a week before Thanksgiving, when I saw a well-dressed, middle-class woman, probably in her mid-forties, shopping in the meat department with her son. Her son appeared to be about fifteen years of age. At the same time, I could see that they had come from a nearby barber shop because the son had these words shaved boldly on the back of his head, "SPACED OUT." My first thought was what kind of mother would allow her son to have a demeaning phrase spelled out on the back of his head? I wonder what our legendary forebears would think if they saw us today. Would they see us as confused? I refuse to believe that anyone wants to be spaced out. Are we so materialistic that we are more concerned with our possessions than with our lives and our children? Are we too busy with our materialist goals to develop our children into good leaders?

Many have surrendered their responsibility for raising their children to television, electronic games, the Internet, and Hollywood. For example, I know of a single mother in her mid-thirties. She has a two-year-old daughter who is very smart, but the mother's focus is not on nurturing her daughter's intelligence. Instead, this mother is concerned about the size of her two-year-old's butt. This mother called her friend in an angry and disappointed tone, afraid that her daughter might not grow a big rear end. There is more to a female than her body! At the age of two, this child should be learning her alphabet and numbers. The question becomes, why is this mother spaced out? This is not how people should think. This mother suffers from some kind of self-delusion, not knowing who she is or what her purpose is. Somewhere in the mother's life, someone told her that her body is all she needs to get by in life.

Anytime you are categorized as the minority or the poorest or whatever in a sense of lack, there is certainly no room for mistakes. There was a time when our test scores were the highest and everyone was competing against us. There was a time when we created most of the inventions, including the ones that we did not get credit for. We kept on pushing and pushing until, heaven behold, the Democratic Party saw that we were flourishing and realized that they needed us lost and spaced out. Then came the late thirties and the midsixties when they got their wish; we started looking for help because many of us were too scared to pursue our dreams and help ourselves. They started giving us benefits, enabling us to stop expanding and growing. The Democratic Party became our home, our existence, and our leader of the newfound world of the Depend-o-crap Party.

When I was in school, I was taught how to look and dress for a job interview, but I was never taught how to work for myself. That skill I learned from working with my father. All students should have more options offered to them and the training needed to become business owners or CEOs, along with how to build wealth and independence for themselves. If you teach a child to reach with high expectations, you will get a better result than if you instill no such guidance. Right now, we are teaching our children only to prepare for the job market; but when that goal is not met, there is nothing left but poverty and government assistance programs. Raise the bar and start teaching them about business, marketing, finance, and management, along with the other subjects. Right now, most of these Democratic Party physicians are trying to turn our children into patients in the party's school system, rather than preparing them for graduation and college. This is essentially a trap for failure. Let's face it, the Democratic Party physicians know this, all of them—the post-civil rights leaders, many of the local pastors, many of the school counselors, and all of the other physicians and providers of the Democratic Party—who desire power and wealth at our expense.

Even some of the Republicans knew, but since our parents and many of us deserted them, how can you truly blame them? Every time the Republicans try to comment on our condition in order to educate us and look for solutions, too many of us call them racist. All of us are in agreement that there are problems in the Black communities, and if all of us are not working simultaneously together in our own homes, we are working against each other individually and failing our youth. Who knows? One day when our children get older, they may run into one another, and I hope their encounter is productive enough for both of them to grow from it positively, no matter what their color may be.

We have to be very careful about what we expose our children to. The contagious lifestyle and trends of those in Hollywood, the television, movies, and videos have been infecting our children's minds for years. The Democratic Coma of the entertainment world is a trap to dumb down our children—the rappers, singers, movie stars, movie directors, CEOs—they all set the trends, and most of them that build a relationship with the Democrats set traps for our children. They tell them how to act, dress, and talk, what to buy, and whom to listen to. Most of them in Hollywood who set the trends do not believe in God. The things that they are teaching our children are without substance and cannot sustain them during the hard times of life.

Most of everything advertised is based on sex; as a result, many young people feel that it is okay to dance naked in videos and shack up. This is a prime example of not being properly taught. Our leaders continue to fail in guiding our youth; in fact, today's liberal parents were failed by these leaders when they were our youth. We need our girls to become strong women; they hold the key to family. A large amount of responsibility is on their shoulders to choose a career and then the right husband and father for their future children the first time around.

This Democratic virus has us in a coma of not knowing whom we should support and whom we should stop voting for. These people insist on treating us like patients. They would rather maintain our problems than help us find a cure or prevent an injury from ever happening in the first place. This is the brainwashing and the confusion of Hollywood physicians and providers. We have to wake up and start supporting the people who are best prepared to enhance our lives and our families' dreams and hard work. Let's face it, we do not need the Democratic Party to validate our existence; we have always existed, but we have never accepted it because we have been programmed to believe we do not. We do not need any leaders or politicians to go out and report the news to us; we are intelligent enough to do it ourselves.

I, too, know the Democratic Coma can be very hard to resist. This Coma is the treatment we get by becoming their lifetime patients and guinea pigs who will never be given a cure. They have had us walking around every year as if we are spaced out, waiting for them to say, "Go vote," to get us to rise up long enough to vote for them again, and again be injected with their infecting policies for expanding this modern slavery. They hope we line up in single-file lines, one by one at the voting place, their emergency room, hoping to get shocked and revived by the voting machine, a defibrillator, just long enough to vote straight Democrat.

The Democrats have already accomplished spreading the virus of fear by devaluing the man's role in the home. A man's responsibility is to house, feed, and clothe his family, but if you give the mother welfare, what role does the father play or what will he do when he is kept from having a second chance at doing the right thing? When you are out and you hear some mother say things like, "I don't need a man," you understand just what damage has been done. The physicians of the Democratic Party have become her man. Mothers, do not let them screw you out of a future with good family values, dignity, and purpose. How can a child expect to have a man for a father if the Democrats are deliberately screwing around with their mother? You see, I have nothing against a mother trying to do the best she can to provide for herself and her children. I was once raised on some of these programs, but when the government purposely manipulates and provides no alternative for the mother, she eventually becomes addicted to the system. Democrats know this and continue to promote these programs. When a person depends on any person or thing other than God, then that person cannot be independent.

The Democrats have even tried to take credit for freeing the slaves, but it was the Republican Party that was directly responsible. Yet the Republicans have faced a great amount of criticism from Blacks throughout our history. It was the Republicans that tried to protect our freedoms and liberty dating back to the 1700s. If the history of this country is researched and taught correctly, the truth will come out and rid us of this Coma. If you cannot believe me, please search for yourself.

Our Hindrances

If a person says to you, "We can't go anywhere until we deal with this race problem," is this person helping you or hindering you? If a person tells you not to worry about a job right now but to collect your unemployment because it is the fastest way to create jobs, is this person really helping you or hindering you? If the Republicans pass laws to allow freedom so that you can go out in the world to make a better life for you and your family, accept it and do it. If they took a chance on losing their lives and the lives of others fighting with you and for you against the same people who want you to remain slaves, give thanks. I ask, "Did the Republicans help you or have they hindered and infected your growth as an individual?" This Democratic Party has infected our lives and crippled our future with no chance of a cure.

God gave each of us a mind to use to improve our own lives by thinking of better and faster ways of getting things done through our own inventions and productivity. The conservatives of this world focus on freedom and liberty, on the improvement of life and jobs, and on investment in real estate, stock markets, and insurance, starting and building businesses and prospering. Is this a hindrance or not? We must not continue to barter our freedoms away to become a dependent; too many people have died for our freedom. As long as we are in this Coma, the Democrats will target us and market their products of fear, racism, dependency, and welfare programs to sell to us until we become hopelessly addicted. As you have read, there are institutions created to house you as slaves and cripple you with no chance of rehabilitation. Hindrance or help? Do we enjoy being confused and brainwashed in a Democratic Coma, a Democratic experiment that controls our freedom and individual vote?

Look at it this way, the Republicans have always fought to protect free men and to remove the racial divide between Whites and Blacks. They enacted the Civil Rights laws in the 1950s and 1960s over the Democrats' objections to them. In the 1858 presidential debates on slavery between Republican Abraham Lincoln and Democrat Stephen Douglas, it was Lincoln who won those debates, and as a result, he became the president of 1860 who passed the Thirteenth, Fourteenth, and Fifteenth Amendments.[1] On the other hand, Stephen Douglas's Kansas-Nebraska Act expanded slavery, and the 1857 case of Dred Scott, a slave who wanted his freedom, are mainly what sparked those debates and led us into the Civil War.[2] The Republican Justin Morrill created and introduced the Morrill Act that the Democratic President James Buchanan vetoed, but Abraham Lincoln signed it into law on July 2, 1862. It was re-signed in 1890 by Republican Benjamin Hayes, which led to the funding of the Historical Black Colleges and Universities. Think about it. The Morrill Act gave land and money to establish many schools in the Confederate States.[3] The Republicans started the NAACP to counter the racist practices of the Democratic Party.[4]

In 1963, A. Philip Randolph, a Black Republican, organized Dr. King's march on Washington. The Republicans fought against slavery and amended the Constitution to grant Blacks freedom, citizenship, and the right to vote, and they pushed through much of the groundbreaking civil rights legislation from the 1860s all the way up through the 1960s. The Republican President Dwight Eisenhower sent troops into the South to desegregate the schools. He appointed Chief Justice Earl Warren to the Supreme Court, which resulted in the 1954 *Brown v. Board of Education* decision. Although some would say Democratic President Lyndon Johnson was the one who pushed through the civil rights laws of the 1960s, it was Republican Senator Everett Dirksen from Illinois who wrote the language for the 1965 Voting Rights Act and crafted the language for the Civil Rights Act of 1968, which prohibited discrimination in housing.[5] In 1983, Republican President Ronald Reagan made history when he signed into law Martin Luther King Jr.'s birthday as a federal holiday, making it the only one that has ever celebrated a Black American.[6] In 2003, President George W. Bush approved the five-hundred-million-dollar National African-American Museum that is set to open in 2015.[7]

These actions by the Republicans are some of the many things that have helped us prosper. Compare them to the many things done by the Democrats. I ask you, hoping that many of you will do or have done the same research, "What has hindered many of us in America? Is it the Coma of the Democrats or the Republican's belief in the Constitution?"

5
Their Curse: The Failed Legacy

Failure – a state or condition of not meeting a desire or intent.

—Wikipedia

Great men are not always wise: neither do the aged understand judgment.

—Job 32:9

Like the fall of Babylon in the book of Revelation, the kings of the earth failed, disobeyed God, and committed adultery. Just like the followers and children of the Civil Rights Movement and the post-civil rights generation, they failed to fulfill the objectives of their legacy. It appears that those civil rights pioneers who fought and died in the struggle for freedom died for nothing. Their agenda failed because many who should have continued the civil rights' "Dream" switched to the Democratic Party and gave them the approval to expand a new kind of slavery. Most of those who followed were never leaders. So many of them went off to be led by what seemed to be images of Dr. King's message. However, it became more like a Ku Klux Klan doctrine that preached the re-creation of slavery. These leaders went off, hoping to one day possess King's popularity but not his "Dream." Many of them used the civil rights legacy to create businesses or political careers so they could use that same doctrine on the people. They have used every tactic they could find to profit from their own kind. They helped to create school programs like the Work Study Early Release, Vocational Education, Job

Corps, and others to help our youth find jobs but never to help them discover their gifts.

They have offered nothing about starting and running a business. In fact, the only time most of our youths have ever operated a business was in high school, working at McDonalds or Burger King as managers. Not only have they failed us, but they have also allowed the experiment on us to continue by helping others to create social programs that keep Blacks under control. I wonder what is next. Jesse Jackson Jr. says, "To end the unemployment crisis, we should change the Constitution so every ghetto child gets an iPod and a laptop."[1] They do anything they can think of to keep us from working on our gifts and pursuing our dreams. They have used every method to keep us on the bottom, even training us to think that the Republicans have never embraced us.

The great Al Sharpton and Jesse Jackson Sr., the so-called Black leaders, are in the business of racism. The more they keep you talking about it, the more inferior and dependent their audience becomes because they do not keep it real or keep hope alive. Both of these gentlemen are reverends, but they hardly ever speak about God unless they are most likely paid by a church to give a speech. When the Democrats and the DOJ were attacking the Catholic Church because it refused to give out contraceptives, they said nothing.[2] Even when the Democrats and the DOJ spoke on rounding up the Black pastors to brief them on what they could and could not say in their churches before the 2012 election, they said nothing. [3]

Jesse Jackson Jr., John Lewis, Maxine Waters, and others are politicians of the Democratic Party who help create policies that support poverty in the party. Many of them have been in politics for at least twenty years or better, and Black people still have not evolved. Tavis Smiley and Cornell West could be right but contradictive; they speak on poverty but are fearful of addressing the subject to the leaders who are in charge of the expansion of poverty. Yet, they market themselves in their latest book, *The Rich and the Rest of Us*, as though they are poor. Which is it? They cannot act as though they are helping poverty when they profit from it at the same time.

Most of the children of the legacy seem confused, and none has become a leader. For example, Martin Luther King III followed Al Sharpton to Washington, DC, in 2008 for the March on Washington and other places, and we can see where that has gotten us. Bernice King followed Bishop Eddie Long of New Birth Church in Atlanta, but he needs leadership himself. Bishop Eddie Long was involved in a sex scandal with five young men who attended his church when they were younger. Since then, they have worked out an undisclosed amount for a settlement.[4, 5] Then there is Dexter King who moved to Los Angeles allegedly to start an acting career. My heart goes out to them, but when will they stand up and fight·for their father's legacy? Were we better off during the era of the KKK? At least before Dr. King died, we were fighting against them; now we have joined them with these false leaders leading the way. How long will we continue to let these so-called leaders abuse the movement and the legacy? I would rather see his children standing up for the legacy than let the false leaders destroy it.

Andrew Young, President Obama, and many other Black so-called leaders know who has failed Black Americans; they are just not interested in the solution. They are interested only in the profit they make from their back-door negotiations when we march for them. The more we march, the more their pockets resemble the mumps. This list continues to go on and on about the failure of the legacy.

Failing America

Many might ask, "Why Obama?" But if it were not for our emotions and hopes for a Black messiah that has protected his failures, we would have seen this coming. All I have heard is, "He didn't start this; it was Bush," but even I know better. In 2003, when the housing market was starting to collapse, President Bush called on Congress for help in creating a system that would regulate and reform Freddie Mac and Fannie Mae, but the Democrats refused, even blocking it from passing. Even the then Democratic chairman of the House Committee for Financial Services, Barney Frank, did not want to act on saving the crisis. He actually encouraged more lending.[6, 7] In 2006, Congress was controlled by the Democrats in both houses, the House of Representatives and the Senate. Bush called them in to figure out what to do with Freddie and Fannie, but the Democrats refused to do anything.[8, 9] Neither of the two houses responded to President Bush's demand to resolve the crisis, so there we went into the biggest housing crisis America has ever seen. The Democrats had enough power to save Freddie and Fannie in 2006 and could have saved this country from this depression, but instead, they did nothing. They have destroyed it just to destroy President Bush's legacy. You have to understand how the process works. A president can do nothing if the opposing party controls one or both the House and the Senate. After all the complaints about Bush, three years later with three stimulus packages from President Obama, we are still in the same predicament, only worse.

In a September 16, 2011, article from *The Hill,* Mike Lillis reported California Representative Dennis Cardoza of the Democratic Party as saying, "President Obama's administration has gone AWOL on this issue of the mortgage crisis," and, "The American people are suffering from mismanagement." Even Joe Biden, President Obama's vice president, said, "Even though 50 percent-plus of the American people think that the economy tanked because of the last administration, that's not relevant. What's relevant is we're in charge. And right now we are the ones in charge, and it has gotten better, but it hasn't gotten good enough."[10] Not only has Obama failed, but he spent too much money on failed green companies that went under after receiving government funding. Obama had a $787 billion stimulus package that was supposed to create jobs and build infrastructure to save the economy. However, he did what he claimed Bush had done and what Hillary would have done, catered to lobbyists.[11] President Obama gave green companies grants, many of which have closed down after receiving the money. For example, $535 million went to Solyndra, $5.3 million to Evergreen Solar, $500 million to Spectrawatt, $2 million to Mountain Plaza, $10 million to Olsen Corporation. They, like others that received substantial funds from the government in this program, went under and filed for bankruptcy.[12] I would like to believe that this is not true, but my research says otherwise. We have to ask ourselves one thing: if the money did not go to these companies, where did it go? Why did that money not go to create jobs or go to some type of small business program to create small businesses? The more people are working, the more taxes the government receives. Government cannot create private-sector jobs, but it can create a friendly environment for businesses to thrive and to hire more people who, in turn, can take care of their families.

Our Parents' Failure

As I look back, our parents failed us as well. They thought that we needed these leaders, not realizing that they were capable of leading themselves, their families, their future, and their children. Many of them thought these leaders knew more because they were talking loudly but saying nothing. Our parents failed many of us by giving up their role as leaders to these false leaders. They failed to protect and defend us and failed to keep our families together. Most of our fathers failed to guide and teach us, the future generation, on how to use our gifts to accomplish our goals and to become self-sufficient and independent. Our families wanted to become strong, but they started believing the inspiring speeches of false leaders. They embraced them, protected them, and defended them. Today many of these same men, who failed to fulfill our historic legacy, ran away from their responsibilities to become the fallen legends of this post-Civil Rights Movement.

Since the assassination of Dr. King Jr. in 1968, most of the Democratic males of that era became too scared to lead, gave up trying, and ran away to surrender to their own spiritual assassination. Most Democratic men of today are too busy trying to master the game of being slick and forget that there is more to life. Instead of them teaching the young males how to be men, these males started rapping to the girls. This is the exact image of how to be players and cheaters. They failed to be men, failed to be fathers, and so they failed right into the Democratic Coma of the Democratic Party and its experiment. When Dr. King died, our people's spirits died, and they settled for whatever they had, unable to believe that they could truly be free. Many of them were so happy to have the right to vote; yet, they still have not voted. Many have failed to succeed because they were afraid of failing. Some continue to blame their problems on slavery just so they do not have to work to change their lives. We have accepted all of this because we have allowed the Democratic Party to experiment on our beliefs and values. As of now, we still cannot seem to kick the habit. This habit has surrendered values and destroyed most of the Black men's minds and left most of them confused and delusional, unable to function at their best. Some of us will never change, and others will always have some type of Democratic withdrawal.

In 2010, in a local barbershop in Atlanta, Georgia, my point was proven. While waiting to get my hair cut, there was a man, or shall I say a male, I call "Falling Legend," who was suffering from one of those withdrawals. He was debating with one of the barbers about why the Civil Rights Movement was lost. The barber told him that Falling Legend's generation was the reason why Blacks continue to struggle. He said, "We are the lost and confused, and if they would have stayed in the home to help the single mom, things would be different." I added, "Most fathers today have no idea what a man's responsibilities are because their fathers walked out on their children, and today the same cycle continues in almost every Black community. No home should be built on a foundation of a single mother; it should be built on a family man." Since those times, the so-called man has lost focus and allowed his woman to love a new man, the govern-man, a.k.a. the government. This government began to govern men who would not govern themselves or their families. This government is the Democratic Party that disabled many from fulfilling their responsibilities to their family. They provide housing, food, clothing, and welfare, everything that is required of a man, husband, or father.

That After-the-Civil-Rights-Proclaimed-Soldier made every excuse why he had not been there for his children and why he was not to blame. He stated, "My children know I love them." I proceeded to ask him, "Why would any man walk away from his images and responsibilities?" I asked him, "What type of advice would you give to a young father?" he replied, "There are things that you just can't tell, you just have to figure it out for yourself." I replied to his statement, "You are not a wise man, just a man with a failed idea." We went on talking about the difference between the generations, and he asked me if I knew the CODE. I replied, "No, what CODE?" Falling Legend headed towards the door and repeated, "There are some things you have to figure out for yourself," and walked out. It is clear to me that this male is not a wise man, but rather a failed one. What I do know is that there are males like him who call themselves men. This kind of person has nothing to offer. As he was leaving, I said, "Our young people are dying from the lack of knowledge while he claimed to be wise by withholding some bit of information that could save someone's life or possibly some desperate young father's vision. Just because a man is older doesn't make him wiser. Any wise man who is not willing to help another is not a man; he is just a male in a man's body."

It is males like that who are still hanging around barbershops and other places listening to the younger generations discussing what went wrong with the past. Most of them do not know what went wrong themselves. Some say that they were the wise men of the sixties, but were they wise? Wise men share and pass down important knowledge to the young. I say, "Just being older doesn't make them wiser." How can you determine if a man is wise if he never opens his mouth to share his wisdom? We cannot be fooled by those who claim false experience and those who claim they saw it but were never there. We have to stop sitting around hoping that the government will one day give our children hope, a scholarship, and teach them how to save their money. Our children need the best that we can give them, not what someone else has promised them. If our children cannot get into college, it is because we—and not the government—failed them. We failed to prepare them for their future. The government owes us nothing; we owe it to ourselves and our children to provide them with the best experience. Before calling yourself a parent, you must decide what is it that you are willing to sacrifice. You cheat yourself by lowering the standards; you treat yourself by raising your expectations and getting what you deserve by working for them.

The Failed Soldiers were willing to take anything the government gave their children as long as they did not have to do for their children themselves. We have become what most politicians want us to be, dependent because one group thought Blacks could not make it on their own without government assistance. To this day, many of them have not realized that we are free, and they think we are still trapped in the same slavery conditions of dependency and failure to find purpose. The new leaders of today do not want you to know the truth because you will wake up realizing that you no longer need them and their promises of dependence.

Many of us wait patiently in hope of receiving wisdom from them when they have no wisdom to offer.

During another episode with a more unusual Failed Legend of his time in 2010, I had a phone conversation, or shall I say a debate, with him about the odds of playing football versus becoming a lawyer. He said one of the most ridiculous things, "It's ten times easier to become a quarterback than a lawyer." I almost fell out of my seat when I heard him say that. Over 90 percent of most parents that have boys encourage their sons to become athletes rather than doctors or lawyers. The odds of having that football dream come true is one out of fifty thousand. If you have everyone fighting for the same goal, it decreases the chances of playing ball. If your life is decided by a panel or others selecting you, you are not in control of your future; someone else is. Being a lawyer, doctor, teacher, engineer, or a restaurant owner is totally your decision. It can happen if you want it badly enough and are willing to work to make it a reality. Becoming a lawyer or doctor is not decided in a draft. If you study hard and do the work, that knowledge is yours. Then you have chosen a life instead of a trap set for you to fail. You do the work; you pass. Greatness comes from within, and many great players are not chosen because there was not enough room to enter the league. This is why it is very important to pursue your academic studies just so you will have something to fall back on if playing ball fails.

We must understand that it takes a smart man to possess the right amount of wisdom and intelligence to share his deepest, greatest thoughts and understanding in order to help another person. A male that has just existed is called a male, human being, or person of the male species. But a male that is responsible is a man who is willing to stand up for something or die trying. A man that is willing to learn and share his understanding is a man that lives not only for himself but also for others. This kind of man uses his knowledge and wisdom to determine his future. Wise men can be afraid, but they do not let fear control them. They teach their children everything they know so that one day their children will use this wisdom. This starts a prosperous cycle of the older generation teaching the next generation. Having an understanding that is exclusive to one person has less value than the person with a revelation that is shared. It is not until he shares it with others or puts it into action that the value is determined. A man can never be called wise until he is heard or judged by others. I say, "A man is better defined in the eyes of another than by the tongue of himself." Wisdom is demonstrated when you have good understanding and judgment in a situation.

As I looked back to understand the effect of this Coma and how the Democrats have implanted this mindset for us to fail, I found that many of us have also failed to know God. We put prayer first without taking action to carry out God's will and then claim we gave it our all. Praying is not all we have; trying is all we have left. I have watched many of us spend more time on our knees then on our feet trying to make something happen. I have heard many of us ask God to lead but never respond to the instructions from God. How many times are we going to pray for help if we will not follow the instructions? Praying without trying is hopeless. We are God's instruments on earth. He uses our hands and feet to carry out His will.

It has become a test of whether we can accept our lives where we are today or where we have not gone to understand our purpose tomorrow. No matter what we have been told, we were not born for nothing. Our lives as human beings are too valuable to spend sitting around thinking that we do not exist and our talented hands are worthless. I say to you, the man of the house, choose God so you will find yourself to save yourself and your family. Ask Him to show you how to become responsible, to show you how to be a provider and a protector, and to show you how to break the bondage of the shackles from around your feet to save your family from this Democratic Coma.

Trying has been my strength all my life, even at an early age when it should have been explained to me why I felt different. I knew I was blessed with a gift; I just did not know what to do with it. At an early age, around eight, my uncle offered me the benefits of being baptized, and my father concurred, but neither one of them explained to me the importance of knowing God. I was told to get baptized, but they never told me why. Afterward, when I was asked how I felt, I said, "The same, nothing's different." It was not until I was older that I figured out the answer. The problem with life is that there are so many people who think they are wise but have not gained wisdom, let alone received any understanding. There are those who will tell you what you should do just to say they told you something. Most people will never tell you why you should or should not. Most times, they themselves do not know. Learning from experience is good; however, some people are not paying attention.

As I sit here watching the falling of the Black community right before my eyes and how we are failing to grasp all the opportunities and possibilities for us to become great, it makes me think. When will we celebrate the legacy and live by the "Dream"? Many have died for us to have such a life. We cannot continue to fail our youth as though we do not care. How long will it take us to wake up before we remove ourselves from being under this experiment for failure? Our youth are in the party's Coma, and we must liberate them. We must apply some pressure on the so-called leaders because not doing anything about them is like preparing every youth to fail.

6

The Leaders: Gradually Selling Out

For the leaders of this people cause them to err; and they that are led of them are destroyed.

—Isaiah 9:16

Leadership – The process of social influence in which one person can enlist the aid and support of others in the accomplishment of a common task.

—Wikipedia

Those who desire to serve the Negro people must be prepared for criticism from his own race.

—Marcus Garvey

I have come to only one conclusion. In order for Black Americans to come up, their false leaders must come down. One of the main reasons Black Americans have had so many setbacks in their lives is their choice of people to lead them. Since 1965, we Black Americans have encountered dozens of self-proclaimed leaders that have acted like dictators from other countries. They have told us what we should think, what we should do, and how we should live our lives. These leaders have acted as though they know what is best for us, and they have acted as though they speak for us all.

Such leaders around the world are called dictators. In China, the ruling committee created a One Child Policy in an effort to control the population, and in many parts of China they have outlawed the practice of any religious beliefs.[1, 2] In Africa where there is gold and oil, there is also a high level of poverty and much corruption. Their leaders are enriched with aid from all around the world yearly, but the African people continue to fail. This kind of leadership has never been good for people. So why is it that we Black Americans are the only group of people in this free country who are quick to claim local leaders and suffer from them the most? Why is it that those same leaders are the only ones that are advancing and not the people they serve? With so many of them, one would think we were the majority; but still to this day, we have not grown from being a minority. In America, these leaders do not consider our poor as being poor when compared to other countries around the world. To them America's poor are living in luxury through government assistance.

In this free country, we are sometimes critical of people like the Chinese and the Africans. It is interesting to know that most Black Americans are, in fact, denying themselves their own rights and are no better off than those within a communist regime. The difference lies in the way we Black Americans choose to eliminate our rights. Most Black Americans refuse to think independently in exchange for some handouts without knowing that they are gradually selling themselves out. What is it about these leaders that caused them to join the Democratic Party, which has a history of fighting against civil rights? We have to ask ourselves why we constantly choose false leaders who treat us as any dictator would, only under the guise of democracy, mostly by their mismanagement of money and our lives. Oftentimes, the result of one's being poor is that rot sets in where false leaders' corruption begins.

Take, for instance, Rev. Jesse Jackson Sr., a Black so-called leader, whom I sometimes call "The Jekyll," who flourished on scene in search of power at the very moment of the assassination of Dr. Martin Luther King Jr. by spreading his most famous rumor that Dr. King died in his arms.[3] However, in the book, *Shakedown: Exposing the Real Jesse Jackson*, the author and historical researcher Kenneth R. Timmerman revealed the truth. In an article by Geoff Metcalf, Timmerman said he spoke with Reverend Ralph David Abernathy, the then head of the SCLC (Southern Christian Leadership Conference), and others who had been with Dr. King. They told him, "Jesse was never on that balcony at the time of the shooting. He was in the parking lot talking with a bunch of musicians." In that same article, Timmerman went on to explain, "Jesse ran and hid behind the swimming pool area and reappeared twenty minutes later when the media arrived with Dr. King's blood smeared on his shirt." Timmerman said, "The next day when Jesse showed up in Chicago to be interviewed by NBC's *Today Show*, he arrived with a chauffeur, a P. R. agent" to further market and manage his new career, wearing the bloody shirt that he claimed had Dr. King's blood. Not only did Jesse lie about Dr. King dying in his arms, but they said, he smeared King's blood on his shirt to validate his lie.[4] In the book, Timmerman wrote about how Jesse was confronted and suspended from the SCLC by Rev. Abernathy for taking money from the SCLC during a Black Expo. What a small price to pay to become a new Black leader of the Black community. And what little time to give in mourning a friend's death. How convenient!

During another episode in 1977 when the Community Investment Act was passed by Democratic President Jimmy Carter, Jesse Jackson and ACORN, the same community organizing group that Obama worked for, forced banks to give loans to Blacks and other less fortunate minority groups, knowing they could not afford them.[5] Many have said this could have contributed to today's housing crisis. They threatened the banks, picketed their businesses, and/or called them racist if they did not provide the loans. They would do anything they could think of to force their agenda. Now many of us would think this was a good thing, but when you know a person cannot afford a home, it eventually creates homelessness, one of the worst ways of creating poverty. Some have disputed that Jesse's action could have intentionally caused bad consequences, but since he is in the business of creating poverty and dependency, Jesse knew what he was doing.

After all of my research on Jesse's driven behavior, I started to think about my encounter with him at his book signing in 2000. When I asked if I could take a picture of my two-year-old son with him, he replied with a hesitating yes. I sat my son on the table as Jesse had asked, and he put his arm around my son in what appeared to be a magical illusion. It looked as if he was hugging him, but in reality, he never touched him. For years, this puzzled me; I could never quite put my finger on the reason. I just accepted it as probably being normal for a popular leader who was a servant of the people. My son was clean; in fact, I had just given him a bath shortly before we walked into that mall. I had also just wiped his hands with a nice, scented J.J.'s baby wipe after his juice and crackers. To this day, I still have that photo of a false illusion to keep Jesse's hope alive.

Alfred Charles Sharpton Jr., another Democratic physician, who I like to call Dr. Revernstein but is known today as Reverend Al Sharpton, was selected by President Obama to lead the so-called Black Agenda. Many feel it is to keep Blacks tame and controlled like good plantation Negroes. Sharpton is an activist who surfaced more than twenty years ago in the media spotlight when he went to the aid of an alleged rape victim, fifteen-year-old Tawana Brawley, in Wappinger, New York. The case was later dismissed because it appeared that the so-called victim had lied about being raped by six white men, one of which was alleged to be a police officer. One of Brawley's lawyers stated that on several occasions a local prosecutor named Steven Pagones "kidnapped, abused, and raped" Brawley.[6] One of Sharpton's aides testified that Brawley's lawyers and Sharpton knew Tawana Brawley was lying. In the same article, according to People.com, Reverend Al Sharpton and attorneys Alton Maddox and C. Vernon Mason were Brawley's advisers and had inflamed the matter, knowing that it was a hoax. Al Sharpton's right-hand man and aide, Perry McKinnon, said, "Tawana's defense was nothing but a pack of lies," to which he later added that Sharpton privately agreed with him. McKinnon, one of the strongest witnesses, is on record, saying, "This case is not about Tawana. It's about Mason, Maddox, and Sharpton taking over the town, so to speak." He went on, explaining they were "hustlers and crooks" and quoted Sharpton as saying, "We beat this, we will be the biggest niggers in New York."[7] Now, after all of my marching in support of Sharpton, I started to wonder how long I had been in the Coma of not knowing who this man really was. How could I have missed this? Even Brawley's neighbors overheard Brawley's parent trying to abort the plan.[8] Al Sharpton was ordered to pay his share of a $345,000 judgment to the local prosecutor Pagones for falsely accusing him of the said crime.[9] Al's share of the $345,000 judgment elevated his platform, and from this, he declared himself the leader of the community. This event created another setback for poor Black Americans with repercussions even to this day.

In July of 2011, Wayne Barrett of the *Daily Beast* raised questions regarding Al Sharpton's agenda towards the very people he claims to represent. Al used his face again on another occasion just to promote himself. Many think he used the Comcast deal to elevate himself by orchestrating the merger of TV One and Comcast that earned him seven hundred thousand dollars a year for his radio talk show and his role in lobbying for the merger of NBC Universal and Comcast in order to land him his own TV show. This show was expected to pay him one million dollars a year. Sharpton used his civil rights skills to lobby FCC members. This was a deal that had nothing to do with racism, poverty, or any improvement to advance the Black community. Sharpton sent a letter to Mignon Clyburn, a member of the FCC, and Representative James Clyburn, the father of Mignon, to help him receive backing in exchange for Clyburn's keeping his seat in the House. With all of the collected problems within the Black community, you would think this deal would have helped someone other than them. It was reported that Comcast gave $10,500 to Representative Clyburn and $140,000 to Sharpton's National Action Networks since the deal was proposed in 2009.[10] In August 2011, Al Sharpton was hired as host at MSNBC over many qualified journalists, a position that he was never trained for. Now many of the Black journalists are mad about it.[11] You can call it what you want, but it seems to me that capitalism continues to work for Sharpton but, again, not for the people he claims to lead.

In September of 2011, a listener called into Sharpton's radio show to ask him about the problems against African Americans. Sharpton replied, "We can't do anything until we solve this race problem." Well how long will that take? You see, they will continue to use racism, knowing that it is a personal problem that can never be solved until everyone stops talking about it and gets on with following his or her own dream. Racism is an individual choice, based on his or her family upbringing. You can never stop anyone from disliking you; it is the person's choice under the Constitution. We are free to say what we believe as long as we do not act it out in a physical way that would harm someone. There are government laws in place to punish that behavior, but how can you measure evil intent?

On September 20, 2007, I got to measure those intentions for myself. I went down to Jena, Louisiana, with my ten-year-old son at the time to support the Jena Six. Thousands of us were marching around the community. There were actually two marches going on.[12] My son and I were up front, marching right behind Al Sharpton, echoing his message with my first new bull horn, when all of a sudden there were no more spectators and no more media on the sidelines, either following us or in sight. Al Sharpton, looked around and over his shoulder, as though he was searching for someone and, out of nowhere, took off running and jumped into a nearby SUV, all within a few seconds. The entire crowd stopped in a daze, looked around, and tried to figure out what had happened and what they should do next. They were saying things like, "Where did he go?" and, "What should we do now?" A lot of us had never been to a march, let alone knew what to do. We felt abandoned and left without a clue. I guess when the media go, the leaders go ... back to find another crowd and another way of marketing themselves.

Now, was he running because there were no more media, or was it all a part of advertising and marketing, just to say he was there? And why were there two marches less than five minutes apart? Al had one, and Jesse had the other. They both spoke on the same stage to almost the same crowd. There were two agendas. Which speech should the people follow, and which one got paid? If you go back to research these events, nothing got done; it was just a photo op for the "leaders" to say they were there. You see, Jesse and Al cannot find a place in politics to run their business of racism, so they hide behind their reverend titles just to look convincing in tricking the Black Americans. There will come a time when all will wake up and see the truth about these men. Now they rush to the scene of the Florida case of Trayvon Martin vs. George Zimmerman without having any facts. They were hoping the case was about racism until they later found out that Zimmerman was a Hispanic and a registered Democrat.[13]

Again, they showed up after the crime instead of having programs in place to prevent the crime. To avoid the embarrassment, they changed their agenda to racial profiling and blamed it on the Republican Party. Sharpton and Jackson knew exactly what they were doing. Their plan might have been to help set up more riots to enact martial law. The president and Eric Holder did nothing, Spike Lee and Roseanne Barr tweeted out an elderly couple's address, thinking it was Zimmerman's, so the outraged public would harm or frighten him so he would not testify. The New Black Panther Party called for the capture of Zimmerman, dead or alive. In doing so, all of them put innocent people's lives in danger without having the facts. Let the legal system run its course? We give racism too much attention, power, and credit, as though Blacks do not commit the same crime against our own, causing our youth to be intimidated by Whites in the real world. When a White person does something to Black Americans, we blow it all out of proportion and call it racism. It is very seldom that you will see a White person harm Blacks. But when Black Americans harm each other every day, we turn the cheek or laugh about it instead of reporting it because of some idiotic no-snitch ghetto rule. Crime would immediately decrease if we took crime seriously and came together as a community to report all crimes. It is highly unintelligent to practice a no-snitch policy with those who bring harm to others. Why tolerate people who could turn against you next? This reveals a level of ignorance and a definite lack of common sense and morality, which has worsened problems in our communities. How can you ignore or tolerate someone who harms another and not report the crime and then, when that same crime is committed by Whites against Blacks, let it become major news? In fact, when I lie down at night, I do not picture a White person entering my home uninvited; it is the image of my own race that reminds me to lock my door and check my clip and chamber.

We do not need statistics or the smartest of scholars to tell us that Black-on-Black crime, or shall I say Democrat-on-Democrat crime, is higher than any other crime committed. Black Americans profile each other; Black females probably clench their purses more tightly and lock their doors more securely than females of any other race. Many of us Black American males clench our guns in passing because we do not know when we might be profiled as victims or just simply have to defend our family or ourselves in a carjacking, home invasion, or robbery. If most of the crime is committed by Black Americans, the police have to profile just to keep the crime rate down and protect the innocent. Again, with no jobs, the dismantling of families, no purpose in many of their lives, and no other alternatives presented by leaders, this will continue to happen. The president and Eric Holder are just sitting around without a word, hoping this will arouse the Blacks for the president's re-election while they strike poses to look genuine and connected. Are they sacrificing the lives of voters for a re-election? It seems obvious that Obama does not care, based on his lack of action for his people. As for Sharpton, this is just another Tawana Brawley-type case. If the president and Eric Holder will not do their jobs, this must be a part of their strategy to stay in power. Why would the president divide the country? I remember, when he was running for president, he said he was the "president for all Americans." If so, when will he start showing some concern?

Many of these leaders think that just because they marched with Dr. King it somehow validates their existence. We do not need ineffective leaders; we just need ourselves and some new faces that have fresh ideas and are willing to work with all colors and ethnic groups across the board. That was King's story. How long will we continue to sit back and watch these false leaders advance on our backs? Ask yourself, have you grown with these individuals since Dr. M. L. King died? How many families have they led out of poverty? Any? If so, show me proof.

There is another gentleman, who I like to call Warren Uglyman, a radio personality who flip-flops on issues when it comes to talking against President Obama. Warren, who has his own agenda, likes to use the art of persuasion to get his listeners to think a certain way. Boldly he will tell you, "I'm trying to get you to think a certain way," or, "There's a method to my madness." However, when you do not agree with him, he has a fit and tells you not to call his show anymore. I know from firsthand experience. His main objective is to force you into a trap of ignorance by influencing your thinking and reprogramming you to think his way. With this type of nonsense, I bet, by the time the election comes around, his voice and others like him will no longer be broadcasting on the air.

Manipulators prey on your self-esteem and make you doubt your purpose for existing. Some of us live to find our purpose, but others are unaware that they have a purpose; they just exist with no understanding. False leaders have realized that the majority of us will not think for ourselves, so they have taken the initiative of thinking for us. After the Civil Rights Movement, many of those so-called leaders realized that racism and hope could be a business, so they have created a business of service, beating you over the head with their agenda, issues that were already fought for in the sixties and won.

For example, Dr. Revernstein knows that many of his listeners do not pay close attention to politics; he knows that most of us do not follow reliable news outlets or research the information given. He and others like him know that most of us do not believe that we are free. They know that most of us do not believe that Black Americans have equality. They control us with treats that in the long run will control us: "You don't need a job," and, "The quickest way to create jobs is to provide you with more food stamps and unemployment checks." "It the best bang for the buck," says Nancy Pelosi, the Democratic Speaker of the House before the 2010 elections.[14] Many of us know that she is one of the reasons that some businesses will not hire anyone. On March 9, 2010, she spoke at a conference for the National Association of Counties on what was in Obama's Health Care Bill. She said, "You have to pass the bill to know what's in it." Now who would hire anyone if they do not know what is in a bill that might hurt their business or offset their monthly and yearly projections?[15]

What they have not told us is the IRS will oversee the Obama Health Care Bill. Their plan is to hire at least sixteen thousand more people to oversee this project through the IRS.[16] The IRS will monitor our banking accounts to see how much money we make to determine what health plan we are eligible for. It is said there will be a health care board put in place to determine what type of care we qualify for. In other words, they may get to decide who lives, who dies, and who will receive a transplant or some major surgery. Since when did a tax collection agency qualify to make decisions about cancers, diabetes, and heart conditions? If you do not pay, you will be fined, have your wages garnished, or be placed in jail.

Another bill that was passed and signed by the president and his administration on December 31, 2011, was the National Defense Authorization Act (NDAA), which gives the president and the military the right to arrest and detain you indefinitely without proper cause. The main problem with this bill is that it has the Department of Defense oversee its health care (Obama's Health Care) cost and empowered the military to detain you as long as they wanted if you did not pay or have insurance, amongst other things.[17, 18] Thanks to Federal Judge Kathleen Forrest, this provision for indefinite detainment was struck down. But, what is it about health care that made it so important that it needed military involvement? Since the bill has been passed, many citizens have filed lawsuits against the president and his administration for violating the First and Fifth Amendments. Remember, the overall plan is to have control over you. There is no telling what the Democrats will do next. Sometimes I wonder if the Democrats could get away with implanting microchips into participants or, shall I say, into patients, would they go through with it.

The head physician and the leader of the Democrats, President Barak Obama, who has assured himself of 92 percent of the Black American vote, seems to advance everyone's agenda except that of the people that voted for him. He has signed many pieces of legislation to help overturn the Gays in the Military Law and the Defense of Marriage Act for gays and lesbians.[19, 20] He re-signed the Reparation Act for the Indian Community. He signed an executive order to pass a backdoor DREAM Act for the Hispanics by stopping their deportation so they can continue to live in America and enter college at their discretion.[21] Not only that, the Amish and Muslims will receive an exemption from paying for health care. But all he can give to the American people is more dependency.[22] All of the things that he has given to others are in no way close in comparison to the insulting lack of service for Black Americans and White Americans who have always lived in this country. To them, he offers free cell phones if they qualify to receive food stamps through SNAP (Supplemental Nutrition Assistance Program).[23] The majority of these programs were designed to help people when they are down, but nothing is offered to help them get up and out of poverty. We have to recognize the problem. We are all Americans fighting for our freedoms against all enemies, foreign or domestic, that think they can destroy our very foundation. We cannot let this Democratic experiment hinder us anymore. We have had many presidents that were not the best, but none has done what the Democrats have done to this country. Not only has Obama advanced others, but he has also advanced himself and the friends he has affiliated himself with for what seems like personal purposes and power.

These leaders built their careers and made their money while you and I were not paying attention. Al Sharpton met with the president, and now he has a job at MSNBC because of his political associations. What have these leaders really done for us, other than keep us trapped in the party? If we asked Sharpton, he would say they were just "keeping it real." They use vain words and the fear of racism to keep us in love with them. Just because they say they are our leaders does not mean we have to follow them blindly. It is our duty to find out who these people are, what they believe in, and what they stand for. When we understand the importance of this kind of knowledge, it will become harder for these so-called leaders to use us for their own ends.

My heart pounds with regret, thinking how badly a difference my one vote was making. All I see now in these so-called leaders is failure. An epidemic of hopelessness is spreading throughout America. It has become a deadly one, an airborne disease, destroying all of our hopes and dreams. These leaders do not care about us; they care only about themselves. They need us to depend on them, which means our children will never be free until we get rid of these contagious imposters who call themselves leaders. You have to be aware of this experiment and this game that are being played on the American people. Without our knowing, they have made us a subject in their business laboratory. We are the only group of people that continues to play Follow the Leader down the wrong path to nowhere, hoping to be saved by a man. We have blamed others who are excelling because they choose to think for themselves and choose their representatives with care. Most of our leaders believe that, if they can keep us angry about race and slavery, then we will be too busy to think for ourselves. When it is time to vote, they promote the Democratic Party as though it is made up only of Blacks, and the next minute they promote racism as though all Whites are against us. Which is it? We cannot continue to let them fool us anymore about our history. You must challenge their motives and go back and read this information for yourself thoroughly.

Look at Julian Carr who was said to be one of the most powerful men in Durham, North Carolina, during the late 1800s. Carr was also a private in the Confederacy Army and a philanthropist who gave land to establish Duke University's East Campus. Carr was known for his stand on Blacks being in politics. He made it clear to a group of Democrats after the Black Republicans won political control over the state in 1896. He stated,

> If we can wean the Negro from believing that politics is his calling by nature and turn the bent of his mind into the development of manufacturing industries, what will the end be? It is unlimited. But if the Negro is to continue making politics his chief aim, there can only be one ending.[24]

Do not sit back and let these false leaders keep you from knowing politics, what your rights are, and what principles this country was founded on.

America was designed so anyone can succeed—smart or dumb, skinny or fat—it does not matter as long as Congress and the White House do not change the rules. In America, you can be whatever you want to be, and you can make as much money as you want as long as you are independent.

Some party physicians, like Rev. Sharpton, or Dr. Revernstein, claim to be men of God. Sharpton, however, and others will continue to create a business and a legacy centered on police brutality and racial profiling. Out of nowhere, he has become somewhat of a politician, the kind that Dr. King warned to stay out of politics. Ever since his meeting with the president in March of 2010, he has greatly expanded his profit margin from being in the business of helping people to what I see as the business of racism and dependency.[25]

Why would anyone want to depend on these leaders? Their job is not to help you, but to keep you tame so the money will continue to flow their way from other crooks. Too many of our politicians and activist leaders are the same, not out to help you but to help themselves. Many of them do not want us to integrate with others, they do not want us to know we are free, and they do not want you a part of anything if they are not the ones controlling it. Dr. Revernstein led a march for the Hispanics in New York, and he went to New Mexico to meet with their people in February of 2011, claiming it was for racial profiling, as though all of them are legal citizens.[26] Now if he believes that Black Americans cannot get anywhere until we solve the race issue, then why is he trying to solve the Hispanics' issues? Let me be clear, I'm not against Hispanics or any group of people, but you have to earn your stay and follow the laws to become a citizen just like any other person or citizen who was not born an American. Sharpton is so confident that he has our Black vote that, now, he is working hard to get the Hispanics to vote for the Democrats, too. It is all just a power grab to control more of us.

Ever since the assassination of Dr. King, new leaders have surfaced and made a business out of promoting racism as a product or service, instead of promoting economic empowerment by informing and educating people on how to create patents, start businesses, and create generational wealth. I do not care if they can only promote buying life insurance; at least it can supplement an income. Until we recognize this problem, these leaders will continue to promote poverty.

How did all of this happen to us? First, these leaders needed an agenda that is dear to many and creates dependence—like racism, abortion, rights, etc. They promise to help any group of people with a problem who will not think or research anything for themselves. Their main objectives are to deceive, instill fear, and tell people how much they care when they really do not. They will go behind closed doors to negotiate a deal with the leader of a group to convert the members into voters or guinea pigs for money or position. Once the deal is set, without knowing it, you can be sold off to a new Democratic physician or Democratic scientist for a new experiment. It is all about your vote. Believe me, observe any major group or ask Dr. Revernstein.

Ever since Sharpton met with the president in March of 2010, he upset many.[27] Tavis Smiley was one of them. He and Sharpton had a hard debate on Tom Joyner's

Morning Show that carried over into Sharpton's radio station concerning why Sharpton had not discussed with other leaders the details of the meeting about the so-called Black Agenda.[28] What agenda? There will always be racism because of differences in race, history, uniqueness, and culture, as well as misunderstandings. People like Al Sharpton would have us believe that, by coming together, we solve the problem, but the solution lies within our families, solving our issues with love, honesty, and responsibility. You do not need to be a part of a march to earn the right to take care of your family. As long as you follow these leaders, you will never be able to accept freedom and equality.

Whenever you have different cultures existing in one place, there will always be personal and cultural tensions based on traditions and values. You must learn to accept America as your home and study its laws under the Constitution. Change must come from within; then you may be able to select leaders that reflect your ideas for change. Our children look to us, not to the politicians, for food. The change is up to you to become the leader of your family, the head of your household, and the protector of your future and theirs.

The study of our history will lead us to understand how America operates and what it is based on. You will find that Africans have not been the only slaves and they were first captured and sold into slavery by other African tribes. Although this does not excuse anyone from buying and selling humans or the struggle that our ancestors endured, we see that race is not the problem. The human mind is the issue. It is clear to me that for the last forty-eight years we have allowed these leaders to play games with our emotions and our minds by directing us down a dark path with no light. What we must understand is that we fought these issues long before and won, but we never claimed the victory and moved on. We have equality; we just have not accepted it.

Until the late 1800s, right before the Civil War when the Southern states were discussing withdrawing from the Union, the belief was that the slaves could not make it on their own. Now, if we fast-forward to today, the Democratic presidents—Carter, Clinton, and Obama—still have the same mindset; they accept us as dependents, beggars, and bums, looking for a handout, and we still continue to give them a guaranteed vote. We cannot be loyal to liars, I mean, politicians. We will foolishly vote Democratic no matter who is running for office. In many cases, many of us just vote straight Democrat without even knowing the candidates. We have lost our vision. We were inventors and creators throughout our history, but we have stopped inventing and creating, especially in the worlds of science and technology.

Wake up, and understand!

Some of the worst things that ever happened to poor people were Democrat President Lyndon Johnson's Welfare Act, Food Stamp Act, free housing without limitation, and Planned Parenthood. These programs were put together to defer our dreams and hand over the care and control of our families to the government. Whenever the Democratic Party provides programs for the poor, they are hoping that the poor will not take responsibility for themselves. There are Black American leaders that will tell us that Black Americans are not free and that there is no equality. They are doing this just to have us think we cannot make it on our own. The more we lose faith in our God-given abilities, the more they hope we will stop thinking for ourselves and depend on them.

History provides examples of dos and don'ts. After the Civil War, over four million slaves were freed, left with no education, no homes, no jobs, and 95 percent of them lived in the South.[29] In order to get on with their lives, they started creating, inventing, and improving conditions. Whether it was being an apprentice to Alexander Bell, George Washington, or any one of the American inventors or explorers or great men, they did whatever it took to survive and provide for their families.

One of those men who contributed to the future of Blacks and Whites was a Black American man named Booker T. Washington who taught himself how to read by using an old *Webster's Dictionary*. Later he started his own school, the Tuskegee Institute. One of the most important things about this man was that he was not afraid to work hard to realize his dream. He realized that he would have to build his own school by hand. He wanted the students to learn how to support themselves by planting crops and selling them to pay for books for the school.

Later, in 1896, Booker T. Washington was in need of a chemistry teacher, so he wrote a letter to a young man named George Washington Carver, who had just graduated from Iowa State College with knowledge in agriculture. This was perfect for what Booker T. Washington needed. The two gentlemen did not wait for a hero to save them; they saved themselves. Booker T. Washington and George Washington Carver built Tuskegee with the help of the students and their families. Now tell me, what are we really waiting for?

7

The Party: Celebrating Dependency

As I lay in my bed in what was proceeding to be a cold sweat, I started to think about all the time I had wasted. Think about the time we all spend focusing on everything but our gifts. I pondered one of our biggest failures, the ability to focus on everything but our own purpose. Every year, we look up and count backwards to one to start the celebration of a new year. We look for new prayers for old resolutions and then pray an additional one to solve the old unsolved problems that most of us have been too lazy or comfortable to do anything about. With all these problems happening, I still saw people toasting and celebrating our existence at the bottom of the American Dream because we choose to be recognized as the Democratic Party and not as our unique individual selves.

Every year, we celebrate the new year, hoping that we will have a better life, but nothing changes. I think of the old motto, "If it doesn't make dollars, it doesn't make sense." Somehow, we still are not making enough dollars, and that just does not make sense. Now after all of these years, we have not yet grown into full-fledged and equal members of society. Where is the growth? The party started over forty-eight years ago, and yet many of us are still questioning the "Dream." The question remains, "Have the Civil Rights Movement and its 'Dream' been realized?" If not, we should have recognized these distractions years ago, but our minds were too tangled with confusion and misrepresentations to recognize the truth about the Democratic Party, substituting for modern-day slave owners.

Without a set goal, there can be no true evaluation of real success. And the goals set by others cannot be your goal; each person must have his own individual goal. Goals set within the perimeter of God's laws will benefit all of mankind. The opposite is also true; if the individual's goals are destructive, then all of society will suffer. A person without an individual goal will eventually become a burden to others, and dependency will again prevail. No plan, no goal; no goal, no hope. People without a plan have nothing by which to measure their growth. Dreams well planned will create wealth in all areas of one's life. Having wealth is not always the result of robbing the poor: most people that have become wealthy planned and worked for their success.

This is why we should not follow the Democrats, who punish with more taxes the people who have worked their whole lives preparing to do better for themselves and succeeding. Many of us know that if we had known better, we would have done better earlier in our lives. Planners create opportunities for others while challenging themselves. We all have the ability to do better if we focus on it. This current attack on success is not good for anyone. This approach is like sending our children off to college to work hard so they can have a shot at the best life, and when they get there, we tell them not to succeed. You cannot regulate success or put limits on how far a person can succeed. This is America, land of the free, home to those who see an opportunity and are brave enough to act on it.

Believe it or not, we will always be ready to celebrate the party, but now we celebrate giving them our approval to drive us into a ditch of poverty because we refuse to stand up for ourselves. Our dependency on the Democratic Party holds us in poverty. We know they do not want us educated, but we keep getting sucked in by the government's freebies. We are so dependent on them that we keep turning the other cheek in hopes that no one will notice that we are really bound in chains, wanting to be set free. We are allowing the party to occupy our minds while we ignore the truth and refuse to think for ourselves. Most of us are so addicted to their programs that we have lost all sense of hope and self-respect.

Many of us celebrate our candidates' victories, hoping that our vote made a difference, but in reality, our opinion is not valued. They just want us to vote and smile and keep quiet. While many of us claim to be in the party, the Democrats have been brainwashing and programming us to be the joke of the party. We are clueless about the purpose of the "party"; we would rather focus on what to wear and how fancy we look, not caring that we are broke. No sacrifice is too great to remain within the party. Throughout all the confusion, we made sacrifices to ensure that we are equipped to party with no purpose. So if we expect the Democrats to help us, forget about it; it will never happen.

Let us face it: this party has never been about us; this party is just about the host, the Democratic Party. We are the only ones that do not recognize that the Civil War is still going on. The North and the South continue to fight. The only thing different now is that we, the new slaves, willingly enter the Democratic Party's Democratic Coma. We have been fighting this war since 1861, 151 years ago. We are still in the middle of the fighting but on the wrong side of history because we refuse to help ourselves. No wonder the Democrats have decided to help themselves. They try not to bother us every year, so they settle for the congressional elections held every two years and the presidential elections held every four years, knowing that they really need us to continue their experiment for the grand finale: how to keep the Blacks dumbed down and poor. This party continues to impose their program by giving us false hope. This party has never done anything for us but cost us—our freedom, our independence, our confidence, our talent, our efforts, and our children. Dr. King once said, "The Negro cannot win if he is willing to sacrifice the futures of his children for immediate personal comfort and safety." We cannot be comfortable living lavishly in poverty while our children's futures remain in danger. No fancy car or beautiful home is worth more than investing in a child's intelligence. How long will we continue to sell them out just to stay eligible for benefits?

Welcome to the Party

They say, "The party isn't over until we say it's over." But what if this party was not meant to end? Let me be clear, this party started a long time ago. From the Confederates to the Democratic Party and to the KKK, we continue to vote yes as if we are the new Negro division of the Ku Klux Klan, ready to hang our own selves for a Democratic candidate. You see, when you vote Democrat, you are in the Coma, voting for slavery, not freedom. In other words, we have been in this party voting to kill ourselves. There is a take on a well-known saying: "What's done at the party stays at the party." But what really happened at the party is that we were a part of someone else's dream and not our own. We choose to disassociate ourselves from our own dream. There is nothing to celebrate until we have achieved our own individual success, but if celebrating is what you do, stay sober enough to recognize the journey. Many of us act as though the dream has not been fulfilled when, for some, it has. But for others, they are still in the Coma, dependent and celebrating the life of someone else's party because—as I now know—we were tricked into attending this party.

What we must understand is that the Democratic Party is not like any other party. In this party, they will pamper you and provide you with all the accommodations for free in exchange for your attendance, your word-of-mouth marketing, and always, your vote. Your participation will only help them to enhance, promote, and spread the word about how charismatic and generous they are. You must prove your commitment and loyalty to them by advertising for them; in return, they will give you some of their government's cheese and cheesy programs.

The Democrats offer us what they think would make us want to come back over and over to them—free food, free drink, and even a free gift or some type of free service that could essentially enslave us forever. This pampers us to make us feel comfortable and eager to stay there among like-minded people. However, the hosts control the party and own the agenda to elevate their popularity and power, not ours. They will leave us enjoying the party, waiting for goodies and handouts. If we attended a party with nothing and left with a lot, we would want to go to these hosts' next party. The Democratic Party pampers us and encourages us to depend on it in all things, including our thinking. The most devoted party attendants abandon themselves because they have given up on themselves. The truth is that nothing is free; someone always pays. In this instance, we have given up our freedom for fear and dependency. Remember the theme is trick or treat—the treat is not free, and the trick is a lie.

Each and every one of us is blessed with abilities to acquire and grow wealth, but many of us have not yet grasped the idea. I question, if the party is about us, why have we not progressed? Our children are receiving the worst education, we have not accomplished anything since the 1964 Civil Rights Act, there are more unemployed Blacks than ever before, we stopped creating businesses and became dependent on the government, and we are the only race that embraces being called insulting names by one another and accepts being taken for granted as a sign of love.

Because of this, we have to teach our children to reach for their own highest goals. If they choose to settle for a job, at least they will not be at the bottom with nothing, celebrating hope without applied effort. In Romans 15:4, it says, "For whatever was written in former days was written for our instruction, that through endurance and through the encouragement of the Scriptures we might have hope." Since the beginning of life, God's purpose for us has always been about hope, growth, and prosperity for all men to succeed. However, since most of us have never been taught how to prosper, we will never find hope and will continue to see the party as our only chance of survival. So, if the party is over, when will we focus on prosperity? How many years will we continue to party with no purpose and continue to believe the lie that we have not achieved the dream of equality?

I know many of you have had enough of this Democratic Party, but now you cannot seem to pull away from the Coma. Let us face it, this party has failed us, and as long as we continue to backtrack from the truth, we will always be a slave of the Coma. The Democratic Party has us in a maze running around afraid to break free. We are like addicts going through a stage of withdrawal. Many of us want to leave, but the party has us wanting more. And because of its prolonged use, the side effect is the worst case of dependency. There are mothers who would rather bear the consequences than let go of their freebies. Our fear is that we might somehow lose our security, our benefits. Even those who want more out of life are hooked on the system and cannot seem to break away. So what is it called when you can do for yourself? Freedom! This is what they have taken away, and this is what you must regain. As long as we continue to have dependency and poverty, this party will never be over. Even when the music stops playing, this party isn't over …

8

Intent: Connecting the Dots

Now after sitting down and thinking more intensely about the president, I wondered if there were others thinking the same things like, "Is the president doing his job?" Yes, but not for the American people as a whole. He seems to be taking care of those who have shaped him and helped to create this party game by putting him into office, people like George Soros, "the Brain," a multi-billion-dollar investor, who is also known around the world for taking down banks and economic systems by betting against their growth. Soros is also known as "the man who broke the Bank of England" and for having compared himself to God.[1] Soros said in an interview with Britain's *Independent* newspaper, "It is a sort of disease when you consider yourself some kind of god, the creator of everything, but I feel comfortable about it now since I began to live it out."[2] It has been said that he has destroyed the British pound, and in Malaysia their president called him an "economic terrorist."[3] Not to mention his company, the Tide Foundation, has a reputation for funding terrorists.[4] In 1995, the *New Yorker* quoted him saying how he envisioned himself, "super human since his childhood."[5] He stated, "God in the Old Testament had a number of attributes, you know, like invisible; I was pretty invisible." The Brain has been caught on tape many times speaking on how he has taken down other countries. He has said, "It was lots of fun."[6]

This man thinks that in order for him to become God, he must now take down America and Israel. The only way he can do this is with help from higher up. Soros has stated, "The main obstacle to a stable and just order is America." He has done numerous interviews on TV shows stating his plan, "An orderly decline of the dollar is desirable."[7] In other words, if you debase the dollar, the cost of living goes up for food, clothing, gasoline, and everything. This will cause people to panic and, in anger, destroy property; there will be a revolution in the streets as we have not experienced before. The Brain wants to control the world by implementing the New World Order with Obama's face out front instead of his.

Now I am hearing rumors, like the president is the twelfth Imam, the anointed ruler of the Islamic world, but it does not make a lot of sense.[8] I started to look deeper into this rumor. It is said the twelfth Imam is a prophet and a political successor who is a descendent of the Prophet Muhammad.[8] This myth tells the story of a five-year-old who supposedly had been hiding in caves awaiting to return before the Day of Judgment and the end of the world.[9] Upon his return, he will rule over the Arabs and the world for seven years with Jesus by his side, ready to follow him.[11] This made me laugh, but I did not stop there. As I continued to research this matter, I started to wonder: if this comes true, then what would be the future for America? This would clearly make the president a participant in the wrong-doing against America. This got me thinking. How can we expect the president to create a positive legacy in America if the plan was never to leave one from the start?

When a man believes in mentors or communist influencers like Karl Marx, Frank Marshall Davis, and others, who have spent their lives studying and writing methods of social destruction, somehow, being anti-American is to be expected. Marx, the author of the Communist Manifesto, believed if you destroyed capitalism the government would provide everything for free. However, this may seem right for some people, but the outcome would create a society where no one would have any desire to work.[12] Davis, who wrote the book, *Black Sex Rebel*, about bisexual acts and having sex with underage girls, as a member of an anti-America group,

Communist Party USA, had been under surveillance by the FBI for at least twenty years, dating back to the late forties, for these very reasons. Davis became a mentor to Obama and has been a friend of the family since Obama's years in grade school. In many ways, he molded Obama's thinking as well as encouraged Obama to go to college. Again, I question: if these people and their methods are against America, then what would be the intent for America?

If you recall, when Hillary Clinton was running for nomination as president, she spoke about Obama's relationship with another friend, Bill Ayers. Throughout the primary, Obama claimed he never had ties with Ayers and left out his position as chairman and lawyer of two of Ayers's projects, the Annenberg Challenge and the Woods Fund.[13] Bill Ayers is something of a mentor for Obama. Ayers is known by many as a terrorist and the co-founder of the Weather Underground, a communist revolutionary group known for trying to take the lives of innocent people during a three-day event in Chicago, called the Days of Rage, on October 8, 9, and 11, 1969. Ayers was known for bombing the Pentagon, the US Capital Building and other federal buildings. In an interview with the *New York Times*, Ayers told the reporter, "I don't regret setting bombs," and, "I feel we didn't do enough." According to the *Chicago Magazine* just before the New York terrorist attack on September 11, 2001, Ayers gave an apology to one of the victims in the Chicago bombing, Richard Elrod.[14] This made me wonder why the president of these United States would be closely aligned with this kind of person when, as a child, our parents would have told us to "run from him and don't look back."

Saul Alinsky—another mentor for Obama, admired by Hillary Clinton, a community organizer, and author of *Rules for Radicals*, a book on social revolution—is known for his socialist belief in overthrowing the government by creating chaos and riots. Obama also helped fund Alinsky's Academy (remember, he was alongside Bill Ayers from 1999 to 2002 in

Chicago). Both of them served on the board of directors with a paid salary.[15] Then, we have Richard Andrew Cloward and Frances Fox Piven, socialists who are known for their orchestrating tactics to take down capitalism by forcing society into a crisis by creating a welfare environment that will destroy and collapse the economic system. The idea is to overspend and overload the system with programs and policies that are against growth; however in doing so, this will turn the have-nots against the haves and bring down America. This is somewhat the same tactic Obama used as a community organizer in Chicago while working with Bill Ayers and ACORN.[16] It was there where Obama met Madeleine Talbot of the Chicago branch of ACORN when he became a community organizer after college.[17] From there, he was given a job to train the staff. He did, the Saul Alinsky way. [18, 19] ACORN gained a bad reputation for voter fraud, agitating businesses, and forcing banks to give loans to those who could barely afford or qualify for them because of their very low credit scores.[20, 21, 22] Sounds familiar, doesn't it? After working for ACORN, Obama went to work for Miner, Barnhill and Galland, a law firm that sued banks for not issuing sub-prime loans.[23, 24] It was for that law firm that Obama was one of the lawyers that sued Citibank in the case of *Buycks Roberson v. Citibank Federal Savings Bank*. As of today, this case is on the docket in the Court of Illinois: Court 34 C 4034-Illinois.[25]

Since the start of President Obama's presidency, he now controls the two biggest banks, Freddie Mac and Fannie Mae, that were a part of the scandal and plan to crash the housing market, known as the "Housing Bubble" in 2006.[26] These banks have now somehow managed to get a patent on the device that would control and regulate the amount of energy used inside our homes. The patent for this device was filed in 2002 and approved in 2005. In 2006 when Congress was led by Democrats in both houses, the Democrats created this Cap and Trade legislation, calling it a residential stock trader with complete control of the carbon trade market. The patent for this device can be found on the United States Patent and Trademark Office website, listed as Patent #6904336.[27] Remember, these are leaders that you trust, but this is purely a power grab by the Democratic Party whose members are not to be trusted. Thanks to the Republicans in the House of Representatives, the bill never passed.

Remember, through the bailout, there was a great amount of stimulus money that went to the same two banks, and now the government under Obama's administration owns about 60 percent of those banks. An article from *CNN Money*, on September 7, 2008, entitled, "U.S. Seized Fannie and Freddie," which means they now control them, but the government has still not released any information about what they plan to do with them. If these are the biggest banks and they were the so-called problem, should not the government use the percentage of ownership as power to help stimulate the economy at least by helping the homeowners who are struggling to pay their mortgages? These banks represented about 60 percent of the mortgages purchased over the last few years. Stimulus money amounting to $787 billion, which never stimulated our hands, was handed over to these banks. While we were sitting around bragging about voting in a Black president, the president and all of his Democratic friends were obviously passing our money around, negotiating future deals, and creating programs or projects behind closed doors to benefit them, their friends, and their donors. For instance, because of the 2009 Stimulus Bill and American Recovery and Reinvestment Act, the State of Florida was allegedly to receive $3.4 million to build a tunnel for turtles to cross under a road.[28] In California at Santa Paula Creek, they are allegedly waiting to receive $7.5 million to build a fish ladder so the fish can make it upstream to spawn.[29] Rhode Island has already received their $3 million.[30] This kind of loyalty allows the party to overlook average Americans, especially the less fortunate. This loyalty has been going on since 1877, as I stated earlier, when the Democrats controlled the electoral votes, calling that moment the "Solid South" because the Blacks voted strongly for the Democrats for years without questioning the party about their problems. However, to be fair and balanced, the majority of Black Americans were simply scared of the Democrats' terrorist group, the Ku Klux Klan. Their job was to pressure you into voting Democrat, and in many cases if you did not, you would be killed. Even today, Black Americans are the only group of people who continue to vote with loyalty but gain nothing in return.

Look at it this way, if the government owns a large percentage of these banks, then the banks are controlled by the government. The government has the power to tell them what to do and how to operate. The main thing here is that we need to know what they are doing in order to understand the character of the players. If we understand the players and the rules governing the game, we will be able to understand each play. There has been no transparency as Obama promised; we get to see only what they want us to see.

Remember, the Cloward, Piven, and Alinsky philosophy is to create a socialist society in which you turn the have-nots against the haves, causing enough chaos among the lower classes to get them to hate the haves and the capitalist system. They believe if you impose impossible demands on the government and weaken the poor by using racism to keep them depressed and down, it will cause them to rise up and cause chaos.[31] When enough chaos is generated and the time is ripe, they will, with the help of the discontented, rise up and seize power from the upper class. This strategy is spelled out in Alinsky's book, *Rules for Radicals*. Sound familiar? This is not rocket science, just common sense; if the have-nots, with no training in how to run a business or build an economy, rise up and take power from the haves, America will fall in less than three months. When this happens, where will the people go to find jobs? I never heard of a poor man hiring anyone. You cannot destroy the haves by continuing to raise their taxes without going into a recession, which we are in today. I thought we were supposed to enjoy the fruits of our labor; but without the labor, where is the fruit? How can there be any fruit if you destroy jobs and those who created them?

To be fair, look at the fruit received by the leaders of the Democratic Party. When President Obama was running for president, remember they said he was worth $2.1 million, but as of 2011, he has $12.5 million. Where did the $10.25 million in short-term bonds come from and why are they short term? [32] Does he not believe in his country? Even "physician" Nancy Pelosi's income increased 62 percent in 2011. In 2009, her income was $21.7 million, the following year it increased to $35 million, and as of June 6, 2011, according to NewsBuster.org, she had a reported income of $43.4 million in assets and about $8.2 million in liabilities.[33] Last I checked, this puts both of them in the 1 percent.

Tony Rezko is another one of Obama's Chicago friends who generously shared much of his fruit with Obama. Obama met real estate developer, Tony Rezko, born in Aleppo, Syria, and named Entrepreneur of the Decade by the Arab-American Business and Professional Association, and they hit it off very well. In 2008, Rezko was convicted of wire and mail fraud, money laundering, and aiding and abetting bribery. Rezko was allegedly one of Obama's major fund-raisers and financial contributors that helped him raise money to become senator, along with his fund-raising support for Rod Blagojevich. Reporter David Mendelland of the *Chicago Tribune* reported that Rezko was the key person in providing Obama with seed money for his US Senate seat.[34] As for Blagojevich, he went to jail for trying to sell President Obama's senate seat to Jesse Jackson Jr. and others. Both he and Rezko were charged with corruption. In 2011, Rezko was sentenced to jail for ten and a half years, and Rod Blagojevich was still serving fourteen years. There were many deals leading up to the Obama presidency. Why?

Now we have Valerie Jarrett, from Shiraz, Iran, Michelle Obama's old boss, who is now the chief advisor to the president. In most meetings with the president, it is said that she runs the White House and does all the talking for him.[35] Before Michelle Obama took the job to work for Valerie Jarrett, she insisted that Jarrett meet with her and Obama over dinner; from there, Jarrett took them under her wings and introduced Obama to many of her radical friends, and the rest is history in the making. The question now becomes, "Who are these friends of hers, and how much control do they have over Obama?"

I looked deep into her connections and found Jarrett's mother, Barbara Bowman, an educator and an admirer of Lyndon Johnson's work on poverty, so inspired that she started the Erikson Institute for child development in 1966.[36] Upon forming the company, she hired William Ayers's father, Thomas Ayers, as chairman.[37] Ayers was not only Bowman's chairman, but he also served as chairman and the head for many other companies throughout Chicago, along with serving as vice president of the Chicago Board of Education. In Chicago, Ayers was known as the "Godfather of Politics."[38] As for Jarrett's father, he was a doctor in Iran. Jarrett's husband, Dr. William Jarrett, was the son of Vernon Jarrett. Vernon served on the same union committee with Frank Marshall Davis at the United Packinghouse Workers of America. They wrote columns for some of the same newspapers, and they both were members of the Communist Party USA.[39] Ironically, this is the same communist party that is a part of the Occupiers' war on the rich.[40] Davis would travel back and forth from Chicago to Hawaii, which marks where he met Obama through his grandfather, and from there the mentoring and the molding began.[41]

All of them knew of each other and had been planning this game for years, and because Obama was a foreign student who was of their liking, the Ayers family paid Obama's way through college.[42] In other words, our president got in bed with some radical people. The Democrats are aware, but unfortunately, they know he has to give these people something back. Today, the President's Congress has approved HR 658, the FAA Air Transportation Modernization and Safety Improvement Act that will allow thirty thousand drones to monitor what we do as well as take pictures, drop grenades, and fire missiles at any time. This new technology will give the police a twenty-four-hour high-tech way to profile and act. These drones are scheduled to be up and running by the year 2015.[43]

As you see, these people have had an agenda against the founders of America and their God from the very start, and they have had influence in real estate, politics, education, and on President Obama's future. This probably explains why President Obama voted present on most of the bills when he was in the Senate; he had to remain flawless and seeded for their checks and balances. Now, that Obama has harvested the presidency, I guess, they want us to allow their plan to flourish.

Is this what you want, corruption and people from other countries who are against this country influencing our leaders? If you are not paying attention to all that is happening around us, then get prepared—with our president in front—for a New World Order. This is a world system of government of the wealthiest and most powerful elite of the world using one currency and one ruler. On June 9, 2011, President Obama signed an executive order to begin this system with American participation in the United Nation's "Agenda 21 Program," giving them 16 percent of America to control, a plan that has been talked about for many years with other Democratic presidents, and it seems now we are in its mid phase.[44] If you recall during the presidential primaries of 2008, Obama kept using the phrase in many of his speeches, "redistribution of wealth." Many of us thought that he was just talking about taking from the rich in America to give to the poor in America. That was not all; the alleged plan is to reconstruct America by bringing it down to the level of some Middle Eastern country, which he has aligned America with. Some have even said that this plan is meant to "bring America down to its knees."

If you recall, when he was first elected as president, he went around the world talking to different leaders. During another episode in Cairo, Egypt, on June 4, 2009, he spoke to many Muslims about "a new beginning," outlining the different roles and responsibilities of America and the Muslim community.[45] Many of us thought that he was making peace to mend whatever damage the Bush administration had allegedly done. No, those trips were *said* to be about implementing the New World Order and who will control it. That means the other leaders would have to join and relinquish their power to the United Nations. Much of this plan was drafted when Obama was in the Senate when he introduced and sponsored the bill called the Globe Poverty Act (Senate Bill 2433), which was voted down by many before it was actually passed.[46] This is where the UN would tax every country about 7 percent and that money then would be distributed to help other countries become equal to us here in America.[47] The ultimate goal would be to change the structure of America and take away our freedoms. However, many of the Middle Eastern countries also disagreed with this plan. It appears that the leaders of Egypt, Libya, Israel, Syria, and Yemen were all asked to step down by President Obama in some way. Now many may think that asking leaders in other countries to step down is nothing because America has always appeared as the super power in aiding other countries with food, clothing, guns, money, and protection. But this caused more resentment, violence, and chaos globally. The idea has always been to bring down those who disagree with the plan.

On February 2, 2011, it appeared the call for other leaders to step down was becoming true. ABC News reported that President Obama demanded Egypt's president,

Hosni Mubarak, to step down from power without leaving the people any knowledge of who would take his place.[48] It was speculated that the rebels from the Muslim Brotherhood would step in. In addition, Obama wanted to forgive one billion dollars in debt to the unknown Egyptian successor and give another one billion dollars to allegedly help create jobs and fund protestors with food, guns, and ammunition, knowing that the Muslin Brotherhood has always been America's enemy.[48] Why?

In Libya, Muammar Gaddafi, the Arab president, who once apologized for the Arabs' abuse of Black Africans throughout many decades, said that he thought Libya belonged to the Africans, and that he wanted to do whatever it took to give it back to them. Since then, Gaddafi rebuilt Libya, created jobs for the people, and set up programs to help the country grow, including teaching them how to read and write. He also extended his help to thousands of Black men in Libya and others in America through the Nation of Islam. In 1996, Gaddafi tried to give one billion dollars to the Nation of Islam but was blocked by Clinton's administration.[50]

Even Minister Farrakhan and Rev. Jeremiah Wright disagreed with President Obama on his attack to rid their friend Gaddafi from power. I guess they have to love thy brother, but what happens when thy brother does not love them back? After all, they were the ones who introduced Obama to Gaddafi, and then they felt betrayed. Remember, in February of 2008, Obama denounced the minister.[51] Then, in April of 2008, he denounced Reverend Wright and asked him to remain silent on the issue and step down until after the 2008 election because his sermons started to surface in the media and his public speaking became too overbearing for the Obama's campaigning. [52]

On March 4, 2011, President Obama ordered Muammar Gaddafi to step down, but Gaddafi refused. Gaddafi knew that if he stepped down, it would not be good for the people, especially the Black Africans who would suffer the most.[53] But that did not stop President Obama from pushing the issue.[54] On March 11, 2011, Minister Farrakhan was speaking on WVON-AM 1690 with Cliff Kelley. He was outraged over how President Obama had handled his friend Gaddafi. He stated with a very frustrated voice, "Who the hell do you [Obama] think you are?"[55]A strong choice of words coming from the minister. This was not the only time he spoke out against Obama; there were several other occasions before and after this incident where he became even more outraged.

Weeks later, on April 30, 2011, Obama gave the order to bomb Muammar Gaddafi's home because he refused to leave as the leader of Libya; in the process, it is said that the bombing killed one of his sons and three of his grandchildren, all under the age of three, without Congress's approval.[56] Until this day, there has not been anyone on their side that has spoken on behalf of the innocent, especially the children, a story that many of us were not supposed to know about. A few days later, to smother the past and celebrate the future, they and their media pointed our attention to the president's victory in claiming he killed Osama bin Laden on May 3, 2011.

On August 25, 2011, Minister Farrakhan called President Obama a "murderer and an assassin" for giving the order to bomb Gaddafi's home. The minister went on expressing his feelings for another event. He stated, "That's a murderer in the White House."[57] Behind every story, there is a certain amount of truth; however, in this one, it's called oil. Gaddafi is dead, and now I'm seeing videos of the minister looking somewhat fearful but now in support of Obama. As for Rev. Wright, he has come from retirement doing what he normally does, regardless of what he said Obama told him not to do; talk and preach.[58]After the bombing, lawmakers sought to file suit against President Obama over the illegal Libya War.[59] At least Bush went to Congress for approval before going to war, but Obama refused. Now he will probably allow the

Muslim Brotherhood to invade Israel, our only ally left, all in an effort to create the Arabic Spring, which is controlled by the Muslim Brotherhood. Many believe that President Obama is aware of their plan to control the Middle East and to cause chaos around the world with maybe him leading it.[60]

Now, since the brutal assassination of Muammar Gaddafi and the takeover of Libya by the Muslim Brotherhood, over five thousand Black Africans in Tripoli, Libya, have been retained and/or killed, according to the Association Press on September 1, 2011. To date, the president has spoken out against Mubarak and Gaddafi but has said nothing about the Arabic rebels capturing and killing innocent Blacks and Christians in Libya.[61] The president knows this will destroy the Middle East and take wealth away from the Black Africans; however, he ignores it and clearly refuses to do anything. His support around the world seems to favor the Arabs. Still, until this day, he claims to be a Black American or African, but why have these groups of people not received any recognizable help? He has weakened America and our allies by strengthening the Muslim Brotherhood, the leader of the Arabic Spring. His global plan will destroy America if we do not put the color of his skin aside and wake up to see the truth. Let's face it, the president and the Democrats have an agenda, and only they know what that is.

It is said that Israel is next on the agenda; but if you are a Christian, you will know that, according to the Bible, Israel is to be protected. It is the place of the Holy Land, the place where God promised the land to the Jews, and is the place of His return. It has been predicted by Glenn Beck, who has been on top of this story since the beginning, that Israel and America are next in their plan to overtake in order to control the world. Beck's word has been precise and on point; he believes when Israel goes, America goes as well. On April 2, 2012, the White House held what was supposed to be a secret meeting with the Muslim Brotherhood, until word got out about it. Now, they want the Democrats to help them impose Sharia law on their people or just maybe, the American people.[62] To this day, no one knows all the details of that meeting. What are Obama and the Democrats trying to do to America? Where are they taking this country? We cannot take four more years of non-stop Democratic nonsense when we know the president has promised so many people so many things.

There are other countries that Obama has yet to bother—China, Russia, Iran, Venezuela, and others. On August 18, 2011, President Obama made another demand, calling for the president of Syria, Bashar Assad, to step down from power, according the *Huffington Post*.[63] To add insult to injury, he has also aggravated Hugo Chávez, president of Venezuela, in the same way. Chávez responded by calling President Obama "a clown and an embarrassment who has turned the United States into a disaster."[64] When our top-secret US military drone crashed and was captured in Iran, the president showed very little interest in getting it back. The Iranians see this as a victory for them but an embarrassment for America, so much so that they have now made a toy drone and have said that they will send our president a girly pink one.[65] This event has weakened America's image in the world; now the Iranians see us as no threat. I questioned whether the drone was actually given to them on purpose because Valerie Jarrett is from Iran, but who knows? Almost any person from another country would stand first with his or her country.

Have the Democrats sold out America for this type of leadership to strengthen other countries purposely by weakening our own? On March 26, 2012, it appears that the president did. President Obama made a promise to Dmitry Medvedev, the third president of Russia, and told him, in an effort to send word back to Valdamir Putin, the prime minister and the second president of Russia, "This is my last election. After my election, I will have more flexibility."[66] To do what?

Now, I like to believe he is a smart man, but when the Democrats have a history of doing nothing for the people and the president has not solved the main issues for Americans, what else should I believe? He has done nothing to solve the loss of homes, he has done nothing to create jobs, and his only means to be re-elected is to proudly claim he killed bin Laden. Since, January of 2009 up until now, the US's credit rating has been downgraded from triple A to double A plus by Standards & Poor's, unemployment is up at 8.3 million from 7.8, the National Debt has risen to 15.3 trillion from 10.7 trillion, and foreclosures number 7.7 million. As of today, there are 46.2 million Americans that are in poverty, and 46.1 million are on food stamps. Rumor has it that Hillary Clinton is planning to quit after the first term. Rahm Emanuel pleaded with the president not to push all in the Health Care Bill at once because it might be too much on the people at one time and it might get caught up in the Supreme Court, which it is doing today. So tell me, what else should I think? Do those in this party know what they are doing, or do they just not care?

I see this agitation is affecting other countries with civil wars, spreading like a new airborne disease all across the world. I ask, "How can a man with so much power do so little for the people who gave him 92 percent of their vote?" And to think it was not just Black Americans that voted him into office; others are suffering as well. The president of the United States is the highest power on earth after God. He has the power to do anything he wants, especially with an executive order. So why would the president involve himself in other countries when Americans need help? No other president would have done this. President Obama has changed America, Egypt, and Libya and is on his way to change the world while many of us are playing Pin the Racism on the Republican Party.

These conflicts with other countries are a problem for Americans. The funding for this project was hidden in the

Obama Cap and Trade Bill with some stipulation inside the Obama Health Care Bill. If you recall, when he was running for president, he assured us strongly that everything would be transparent for the American people. Instead, our president, the chief physician of the Democrats, intends to execute this plan at all cost without your knowing. The last known attempt to implement the New World Order was with another Democratic physician, Al Gore. He tried the same thing by preaching the concept of global warming, climate change, or the so-called protecting the environment. Ironically, this plan included the idea of buying and selling energy resources all around the world. Ever since Gore's campaign was made public, thirty thousand scientists have come forth with a signed petition disagreeing, calling global warming a fraud. Many have questioned his Nobel Peace Prize because of this. In an interview with Fox News in August of 2008, one of these scientists, who happened to be the founder of the Weather Channel, John Coleman, and others came out, claiming to sue Al Gore. In 2006, Coleman said he had been trying to get the word out, but CNN, MSNBC, NBC, and other liberal stations would not allow him on their shows. Coleman wanted to settle the debate once and for all.[67] Since the election, President Obama has attempted to push these bills through in pieces. The plan consists of our buying energy in an effort to protect and control pollution around the globe. The government wants to put a cap on how much energy we can use, and if we go over that monthly allotment, we will be charged extra.

The government would take that "extra" from us to fund other countries to rise to the same level as America. Remember Redistribution of Wealth and the Global Poverty Act? You get it. This process will force us to cut back on our usage of water, gas, electricity, etc. This is part of the reason why the Obama administration allegedly stopped issuing permits for American companies to drill for oil in and around America but has allowed other countries to drill in our waters. China will take the oil from Canada, the Keystone Pipeline, which will produce one million barrels per day. Russia will take the oil from the Arctic that is expected to have about eighty-five billion barrels. Both our president and the Democrats have ignored the Keystone Pipeline, even though they know it will create jobs.[68] As of today, the only oil drilling President Obama has approved is a two-billion-dollar loan to Petrobras, an oil company in Brazil, of which George Soros is one of the largest shareholders. In 2009, Soros invested one billion dollars in Petrobras days before Obama made the loan. Now, if I'm not mistaken, is not that called inside trading? How convenient to know that your friend and campaign donor was a short-term shareholder, standing to make more billions. Within four months, Petrobras's shares grew 27.9 percent.[69] How much does the American taxpayer get? Zero! You see, Obama and people like him need their green projects to become relevant when gas and oil prices become too expensive for Americans.[70]

In an interview in 2008, Obama stated that he expects gas prices to go up, "just not so quickly."[71] Why do we have him in office if he is not concerned with our needs? His job is to protect America's best interests, not just his own. His energy secretary, Steven Chu, stated on February 29, 2012, that they need higher gas prices and their focus is not on getting gas prices down.[72] Their idea is for gas to cost eight dollars a gallon, as in Europe. Then we have the president stating on several occasions that oil is a thing of the past.[73] Now, I'm thinking, does he care at all what the prices are? During the president's inauguration in January of 2008, the average cost of regular gas was $1.87 a gallon; but now in 2012, in some states, it is $5.00 a gallon.[74] I do not think the president or any of the Democrats care about the cost of gas and oil for the American people. Their solar and green projects have failed. What is their intention? This party continues to be a complete failure, and now I see the light.

9

Their Media: They Control the Game

Ye shall not fear them: for the LORD your God he shall fight for you.

—Deuteronomy 3:22

Now that my eyes are open, I wonder, why could I not see the corruption in the Democratic Party? Why did I not see these problems years ago? The more I kept searching to find the truth, the more I found that our lives were just a game for someone else. It was played out to condition our minds to think a certain way just so we would vote a certain way. There was no truth in this party; our vote was their only hope to keep the game going. It was structured this way. Many of us know "the mind is a terrible thing to waste." Still, until this day, so many of us have been so deeply satisfied with lies and liars that we have not changed what we have wasted. Many of us may even think, "Our mind plays tricks on us," not knowing that the trick is to play on our mind; this is the game of marketing, the game that the Democrats have put in place.

After continuously researching this matter, the only question remaining in my mind is how did we get into this mess? Have we been set up, bamboozled, tricked, and duked because we do not understand how marketing works? Marketing is structured with the appearance of a game: those who are prepared win, and those who are not settle for a loss. The losers do not understand that marketing is played against those who do not know how to play the game.

In marketing, a buyer, a seller, and a plan are required. This plan is called a campaign. Every day, all of us, whether we know it or not, are a part of a campaign in which we are being targeted by someone who intends to create a level of fear in us or to get us to buy into someone else's product or idea. Many marketers will use some type of fear as a part of their marketing game. Fear is used as a distraction played on the deaf, dumb, and blind by the powerful and the wealthy for their own gain during the game. They need you to support their cause, they need you to be distracted, and they need someone to take the blame when things fail. The people that are always blamed are those that are not aware or informed.

Now, after the many years of marketing and managing musicians in my early twenties, in an effort to get recording contracts for them, I have come to see another comparison with the Democratic Party and the ways this has impacted our lives. False leaders in the Democratic Party use Hollywood and our favorite entertainers to attract us. In the music industry, I watched several artists compromise what was left of their values to become slaves to the executives, producers, and record companies. I watched them play the game of dependency with many uneducated artists by instilling fear to manipulate them. This fear has crippled many artists to the point that the possibility of their having something in the future is almost zero. This fear is only potent when artists have no or few resources to help them protect their welfare and future.

It was during this research that I discovered the similarities between some familiar behaviors in the music and entertainment industry and other characters and behaviors within the Democratic Party. There were the same types of political games being played out, and now, I clearly understand their game of fear, dependency, and marketing tactics used to brand their agendas. You see, it was never the executives' intention to watch out for the welfare of their young artists (any more than the Democrats look out for the welfare of you); rather their intention was to do nothing and then watch the artist fall (as the Democrats watch you fall), knowing that many of these artists did not have proper guidance from the start. As parents, many of us foresee the artists' images rising in fame and then disintegrating, but all the executives care about is the instant opportunity to make money. The idea is good when all benefit positively. In most cases, the industry was never designed for an artist to create generational wealth or to showcase real values for young fans; it was designed to create wealth for the industry and to confuse, mislead, and set up young artists for failure. The Democrats have made us their target; they need us to keep the cycle of dependency going. This drove me to investigate even more into related topics that are similar and presented to us as everyday facts.

They have turned many artists into one-hit wonders or confused, rich time bombs, waiting to blow their wealth back into poverty all over again because they did not understand the game. There are many artists that did not quite understand the game and later lost their lives to the Democratic way of life—drugs and alcohol that destroy moral values for building a strong foundation for themselves and families. Many of the entertainers came into the business with God, but on their last days in life, they left confused about their God. I heard many people brag about how beautiful their favorite's funeral was, but no fan should hope to see a beautiful funeral; we all hoped they would have planned a beautiful life. If death is presented as beautiful, what should we call life? All of us know if the dead could do it all over, they would choose life.

No one could possibly understand or imagine the political influences played in the music industry, Hollywood, and the media to people that are not properly educated about the game. The Democratic conditioning has trapped Americans' minds in a box, not to mention what it has done to the Blacks in America. Making us feel that the only way we can make it in America is through the entertainment and the sports worlds and selling drugs. This game has been used on the same scale by the Democratic Party and their so-called leaders to control their so-called assigned communities and groups to maintain racially divided groups just to keep racism alive. Their actors, rappers, comedians, and singers also know what they are assigned to do and what their donations and support will do for them. At the same time, the Democrats will put all aside to receive it, even if it means selling you out for the support from the gay communities, Hispanics, and terrorists. Why not work for all Americans? These leaders are aware of the problems, but for their own benefit, they remain silent.

So every time a Democratic scam artist has something to sell or an agenda to promote, these Democratic providers will find a superstar to give us their approval. While we stand there watching the balloons floating and the confetti falling on our favorite personalities' faces, the producers of the agenda are gaining leverage and making wealth out of our confusion, lack of knowledge, and confused sense of loyalty. They know that many of us follow the stars for the latest trends, and they know that whatever the stars do, there is a 90 percent chance that we will adopt it because we want to be identified with the trend and the stars' success.

Just to give you an idea of the problem, on October 11, 2011, during a rally to "Occupy Wall Street," a demonstration protesting against capitalism and job creators or what many may call "corporate greed," my research started to unveil what many could claim to be a conspiracy, but I watched it unfold into fact. This event helped in motivating a great number of people to come out and create a sense of chaos, a plan that comes out of the Saul Alinsky book, *Rules for Radicals*. A chaos is created to threaten the overthrow of the government, which can give the president an excuse to call out martial law. This can ensure the president will stay in power because there cannot be any elections while the nation is under martial law. By this, citizens' constitutional rights are taken away.

On January 10, 2010, the president signed an executive order to establish a Council of Governors to govern during a martial law. This council is said to "strengthen partnership between federal, state, and local governments to better protect our nation" at any giving moment.[1] But for what reason? What were they planning to do? This was reported by Alex Newman of TheNewAmerican.com, by MoveOn.org, and by the Tide Foundation, a company that, ironically, is funded by George Soros, the Brain.[2]

The problem with this demonstration was just what I expected: there were lots of anti-Americans and hardly any Blacks that came out to join, so they sent a familiar face that would draw out the Black community. Russell Simmons, whom I had at one time looked up to, based on his background and success in the music business, showed up for the protest. This made me think on Simmons's past. Since June of 2011, Simmons's Visa Rush Card Company has been under investigation for fraud, for charging cardholders a hidden fee.[3] However, Simmons was there, agitating as a liberal, trying to appeal to the crowd as being a have-not. But now, since I have awakened from this Coma, I see that he has expanded into the business of poverty and racism, too. Russell sometimes promotes substandard, distasteful music to the youth; he has become just another physician for the Democratic Party's Democratic Coma.

Not only has Simmons become a part of the problem, but he also tried to expand his income by using the event to promote one of his artists, Kanye West. Mr. Simmons did what the music industry calls a "walk through," which is when an artist needs publicity to promote a forthcoming music project to sell records.[4] The record company will send the artist to a targeted area to gain fans or likeability. Simmons brought West down among a crowd of people that was protesting against the rich and capitalism while he and West pretended to appear like average Joes with West wearing a gold necklace, a four-hundred-dollar pair of jeans, and a three-hundred-dollar shirt and accompanied with bodyguards.[4] This was all in an effort to draw out the Black community for a photo op. As if that was not enough, on the night of October 13, 2011, reported by Jessica Derschowitz, Simmons sent a tweet to Mayor Mike Bloomberg and told him, "I will clean up the Zuccotti Park to avoid any confrontation," all in an effort to keep their names out there.[5] My first thought was, "Why would millionaires be so concerned with people protesting against them and others of their own kind?" You would think they would be protesting him or run them off. The question continues: "Why would a person of wealth support an anti-capitalism event and act as if he is one of the so-called poor 99 percent? There were others that attended the event to attract the Black community: Al Sharpton, Dick Gregory, and a host of others but, otherwise, hardly any Blacks came to participate with the 99 percentile.[5] This still puzzles me because, the last I checked, Gregory, Sharpton, West, and Simmons were making lots of money. The irony is that the people protesting are the very people enjoying everything that they are protesting against, which is called capitalism.

There are more riots and protestors that have been surfacing for a few years now, spreading across the world; the people, threatened by the news that their expensive retirement programs may be taken away to save their nations' economies, are angry. Glenn Beck, the king of research, has said that George Soros and his money are paying for these union protestors around the world.[6] I agree. He got things started overseas and then returned to the US to start things here.[7] In our country, the riots were "created by President Obama," according to Rush Limbaugh on his radio show on October 6, 2011.[8] The protestors are being fooled into believing that the rich and wealthy are responsible for their problems.[9] They should be protesting against the president and his administration, not the job creators. The protestors have been tricked by the Democrats. The president came out in support of the riots and protestors by giving them his blessing.[10, 11] For what? To destroy his country! Some Democrats, including Nancy Pelosi, minority leader in the House, have even given the protestors their blessing. Now this uprising has taken the attention off what the Democrats are doing. The Democrats actually give their support for what could destroy the cities of America, and our president is one of them.[12]

Before you can understand the artificially created confusion, you must understand that there are so many ways to market a product. Take the Super Bowl game, for instance. It is one of the best times to advertise your idea or product because you know almost everyone is watching. The football game is the distraction when, all of a sudden, a product is cleverly presented to the world in less than one minute in a spotlighted commercial. Many of us wait impatiently to see which commercial will be the best, and with no conscious thought, we find ourselves running to the store to purchase that promoted product. The marketers have inspired us to buy into their campaign from the cleverly crafted advertisement.

Hispanics

Now since you have a good idea of how marketing works, let me show you how it has affected our lives today. During the election, we all compared President Obama with Dr. King. For years, when anyone has mentioned the word "dream," we automatically think of Dr. King and the struggle of African-Americans. Once President Obama got into office, one of the main things the Democrats tried to pass was a bill called the DREAM Act, which stands for the Development, Relief, and Education for Alien Minors.[13] This bill, if passed, would provide permanent residency to illegal alien students; it would help them in joining the military and/or going to college for free, and emancipating them in America.[14] The Hispanics, based on this bill, would become America's next middle class if we are not paying attention. It amazes me to know that Obama's priority is to go all out in keeping

Hispanic families together when the Democrats have been destroying Black American families for years, not to mention what they have done to many of the White families.[15] As of today, the Democrats have tried five times to enact this bill, but the Republicans have voted it down each time. For many of us who have not been paying attention, we probably thought that the DREAM Act was for Black Americans when it was really for Hispanics. The Democrats market to us to get our support, based on the act's name. People now call Obama the Hispanic president because the bill does nothing to help Americans—Blacks or Whites. I have nothing against the Hispanics; I just expected more from the president since he calls himself "American." Dr. King would not have singled out one group; he would have tried to bring them all together peacefully. I hope President Obama is not trying to change history by dismantling Dr. King's legacy by creating a new one for himself.

The Power of the Attorney General

Not even Eric Holder, a Black American who holds the position of highest attorney in the land, will do his job. His job is to prosecute and protect the American people against anyone that might be of some threat. Before his appointment to the Obama administration, he actively protected the rights of terrorists, now the Taliban detainees in Afghanistan, Hispanics, ACORN, and other special interest groups, but not the American citizens as a whole. Even on a smaller scale, there are men who were once incarcerated that cannot get a job when they get out. Eric Holder refuses to acknowledge them. He probably would rather fight to ship terrorists from Guantanamo Bay and release them in American streets than to let American prisoners have the right to vote after serving their time completely or help train them so they can get jobs.

I honestly believe in the coming days we will hear more about the White House and the attorney general.

Eric Holder's "Fast and Furious" scandal concerned an operation that put guns in the hands of gangs and drug cartels in Mexico to create chaos so the government could repeal the Second Amendment that allows American to have guns.[16] They could then force people to give up their guns and force the States to turn over their lists of gun owners' information.

Even the Democrats' own Senator Claire McCaskill of Montana has had enough of the Obama administration scandals; she sought for an investigation of the Obama administration's Department of Health and Human Services for giving $433 million to the maker of an experimental smallpox vaccine known as ST-246, that has not been tested on anyone. If so, who would want to be vaccinated first—or at all? You see, the Democrats do not care about American people. What they value is what they can get out of a deal. Remember, there are more rich Democrats than Republicans. "Siga Technologies is a New York company run by a major Democratic donor," McCaskill stated in an ABC news article. "This five-year conflict of interest is the potential waste of precious taxpayers' funds."[17] Their own party is against this deal. You would think this would be a good investigation for Eric Holder. So what is his job, and when will he do it?

In January of 2012, a few days before the Dr. King holiday celebration, Eric Holder wanted to resonate with Black Americans, somehow, by using racism. Holder used quotes from Dr. King's speeches to grab their attention and present support for his innocence in "Fast and Furious." He has not stood up for any issues concerning Americans, especially Black Americans, one of which he proclaims to be. He has not stood up against racism, police brutality, or any wrong that Sharpton claims is a problem for the Black American community. As of today, Sharpton certainly has not held Holder accountable, and my guess is he will get a pass as well.

The Power of This Administration

Eager to know more about other ways this party has been using marketing, I worked my way through documents and websites that reveal many other relationships, one of which is with a very popular company working inside the Obama administration, Google. In some cases, it has been noted that a particular Google executive, Sonai Shah, has been leading meetings, acting as part of Obama's transition team. It has also been confirmed that former Google executives have been playing additional roles. This made me think about all the things Google has been doing with location addresses all around the world and how it could be freely using our personal information. Why would this company be working inside the White House? What role could it possibly be playing? Andrew McLaughlin, the former Google head of global public policy, was appointed as the deputy chief technology officer in June of 2009. If this was not enough, Google executives and employees gave Obama over eight hundred thousand dollars in campaign funds for his election to the White House, and each of Google's executives, including Schmidt, also gave twenty-five thousand dollars apiece for Obama's inaugural celebration.[18] The question is, "Have we been tricked?" What I remember most from Obama during his candidacy was how he accused Hillary and McCain of receiving funds from lobbyists. If you receive funding from anyone, in most cases, the donor expects something back. What type of deal could Google negotiate with this Democratic administration? I wonder what is next in this plan. Many of us may not have paid any attention to this, but this type of marketing has been used as a distraction to take our eyes and mind off the truth of the exact purpose behind the marketing. Make no mistake, in the end, "You can fool some people all of the time, and all of the people some of the time, but you can not fool all of the people all of the time." I hope my personal information from the Internet will not become a topic of a meeting between the White House and Google.

The Power of the President

The major thing that we must remember is this president has the power, but his policies have failed and continue to fail us. His policies will destroy America for years to come and handicap the American peoples' growth. He is using marketing or, in this case, propaganda. We have believed only what they want us to see and hear through the media. Everything in the media is majority-owned or run by the Democrats and their donors. They are providing us with nothing positive that will advance our life and our thinking, only distractions. The Democrats' strategies and tactics are to create dependency and for them to get compensated; and as long as we are in need, they have an audience to market their goods, entitlements, and dependency programs to.

The Power of His God

George Soros, the Brain, the godfather of the media, is one of the richest marketing geniuses in the world today. Soros is an investor and a currency trader who controls a large number of businesses all around the globe. The Brain has built a media empire that exceeds a budget of three hundred million dollars a month to control almost 60 percent of the American media—TV stations, radio stations, websites, newspapers, books, and videos— just to keep his agenda secret.[19] The star that he uses to sell us his product and agenda is our very own President Barak Obama, also known as Barry Soetoro. Soros helped President Obama gain the US Senate and the White House; he has funded the Democratic Party for years, including Bill Clinton's presidency and Hillary Clinton's New York senatorial campaign.[20] The Brain keeps close control of the media, from the *Huffington Post* to your local Viacom radio network, known today as the CBS Corporation.[21]

In the summer of 2002, the Brain spent approximately twenty-six million dollars of his own money to get rid of President Bush. When the Brain could not defeat George W. Bush, he created another campaign and cause: the Shadow Party, which was set up to become Hillary Clinton's administration team, but when Barack Obama's charisma impressed Soros more, it became the Obama administration team. On July 7, 2003, the Brain and others established the Shadow Party made up of his own Open Society Institute members and a half dozen of former President Bill Clinton's administrators and speech writers. All of them came together to form the American Majority Institute, located just three blocks from the White House. A few months later, they changed the name to the Center for American Progress, also known as CAP, which was said to be a research and educational institute to generate a forum for new ideas and policies for Progressives (the American socialists). In reality, it turned out to be an outlet for creating the New World Order, funded with millions of dollars between the years of 2003 and 2007 by the Brain. This organization would be the brains behind the Hillary Clinton or the Obama administration, depending on who won in the 2008 primaries.[22]

In June of 2004, in the New York home of George the Brain, he hosted a fundraiser for Obama's US Senate campaign. It was then that the Brain saw that Obama had what it took to win the presidency in 2008. After that event, the Brain held another meeting, called the "Phoenix Group," in Scottsdale, Arizona, with about seventy of the wealthiest individuals to get them to meet his discovery, Barack Obama. This meeting of like-minded individuals came together to create the most dramatic plan to blow America's mind, especially with Obama being the face of the new plan.[23] You see, what we have to understand is that when wealthy, like-minded people come together to create a plan, it has to work, or someone will pay a very hard price. It was not until March of 2006 that the Brain bought out the mega media outlet company Viacom, which was established in 1971. It included various worldwide cable, satellite, and television networks, such as MTV Networks, BET, UPN, the WB, SEGA AMERICA, CBS radio; movie production and distribution, the Paramount Picture Studio and DreamWorks Studios (which the Brain renamed CBS Corporation, the new "high end side" of Viacom), all of which are run by the same chairperson.[24] Does this clarify why we are in the Coma? They control everything we watch. All of this makes complete sense for why this was happening. This is not about you and me; this is simply about money and power. When a man like Soros who controls people and the media is able to hide the truth from the people and no one says anything, especially the media, you know he is powerful.

Months later in December of 2006, the Brain called Obama for a one-on-one meeting concerning Obama's run for the presidency. Within two weeks, Obama made the announcement he was setting up an exploratory committee with the idea of possibly running for president. Shortly after Obama announced that he would run for president, my research revealed, the Brain started flooding Obama's campaign with funds coming from all types of created organizations set up by Obama and the Brain—the Obama Victory Fund, Obama for America, Obama for Illinois, Inc., Democratic Senatorial Campaign Committee, and a host of other organizations that have not been thoroughly investigated.[25, 26] The Brain is one of most powerful men in the world; if he can control the president, the media, and some of your activist leaders who work for him, what do you think he will do next if you do not wake up?

Marketing against Values

The media, Hollywood, and many politicians have lowered America's values and debased our image. Yet, we continue to give them our votes, buy their products, and raise their ratings so they can gain more wealth and power over us. We allow them to target the weak, the uneducated, and the unrepresented in the game of image media, and we do not protest. They target a person's or a people's image, character, and honor and use it to either build up or destroy for everyone to see. They try very hard to hide their relationship with corruption and corrupt people when they think you are not paying attention, but Heaven holds the truth about the dark nights and shall reveal eventually.

Hollywood and the media will continue to play a huge influence in our daily lives—advertising media, broadcasting media, Internet media, electronic media, publishing media, and social media. Why is it that most Black American radio programs have a comedian or a funny personality to keep you distracted with laughter over everybody's issues but your own? There are so many that use these distracting tactics to create fear and dependency in you when you are not looking. When someone, like Soros, deliberately tries to take over the media, you do not take anything lightly. The president stated in his inaugural speech that jobs and transparency would be his first priorities, but it has been three years during which he has signed almost four hundred executive orders that we do not know about. We do know he has helped every ethnic group but Blacks and Whites who built this country. They keep information out of the media so that you cannot learn much about history and politics except for what goes on in your immediate surroundings. I guess, next, they will try to control the Internet because they already control the media, community leaders, and activists that you all know so well, and it even seems as though they control organizations, like Black Caucus, NAN, NAACP, Rainbow Push, and others. Most of them think they are so sharp. They have changed their tactics to go against what the original pioneers stood for. Without knowing, we have helped them build a fan base from social injustice to social corruption just to elevate their causes and agendas. They are using racism as a business to craft this dependency and to confuse you into thinking that you do not have freedom and equality.

They are meeting privately with foreign and domestic leaders to assist them in reorganizing your country, America. Their action shows that they want America to become a socialist country in which the government controls everything you do, eat, and wear and everywhere you live and go. Whoever is on the bottom will stay on the bottom. Most of these community leaders have their own talk and television shows that promote their own success and that of one man, the president. Our children, based on what they are being taught about our history, will remember only two historical men: Dr. King and Barack Obama. We can never compare the two. Even though they both have a Nobel Peace Prize, Obama's award is questionable. How is it that one promoted nonviolence and equality and the other had us in four military events, which many still call wars—Iraq, Afghanistan, Egypt, and Libya—but complained about and voted against the only two actual wars that Bush had us in. Obama, in his own words while campaigning for the presidency, said he did nothing to deserve the Nobel Peace Prize. I bet he will appear to do more for the people when it gets closer to re-election. Dr. King will forever be in a category of his own as a man of peace, love, and honor. If we continue to leave it up to Democrats, they will destroy King's legacy. We must know the truth about history so we will not waste our vote and the hard work of those who fought for all that we have.

As you can see, fear plays an important role in marketing. The party leaders hope that we, one day, become afraid, panic, and feel pressured to act fast in making an urgent decision while being unprepared and unaware of the whole situation. Marketing has been used to sell products or services. Who knows for how long it has escalated into a tool of outright lying and deceiving to create power and wealth for the politicians and wealth, fame, and glamour for the music and entertainment industry.

We cannot allow others to target us in their campaign tactics to win power and wealth without respecting and honoring us. Their campaign is simply an attack on reality. I am challenging fathers to head home and become real leaders as fathers and men. As long as fathers stay away from the home, there will always be predators preying on their children and wives. This president's legacy will one day cause us suffering because we refuse to hold him accountable today for his actions and deceptions. Most of the leaders today, Black and White, will do almost anything to win power, especially the kind of power that the media protects aggressively for the Progressives' cause.

Have we been set up, tricked, and scammed again? They have repeatedly done this to us: over 150 years of misrepresentation and lies, over forty years of civil rights with no direction, forty years of false leaders claiming they are still fighting for civil rights—to find out later they are fighting only for their own personal greed—and four years of "Hope and Change" that have devalued Black Americans just like the US dollar. They have tricked us to stand on the wrong side of history, making us the laughing stock, rather than a free and prosperous people in America. Today we are the Loyal Confusion of the Black American Culture. We have voted the wrong man into office just for the sake of his skin color. We never thought to measure him, based on the people he surrounded himself with, especially George the Brain, the media mogul. Our existence on this earth has made us confused and lost. But the biggest setbacks that we face in America today are not just the media; they are also Hollywood, the post-civil-rights-activist leaders, and the Democratic Party. They have manipulated our lives to control our thoughts, future, and existence, mainly because everyone wants to be a star, no matter the cost, and everyone wants to have the power, the money, and the respect. In other words, they would rather denounce you than be on your side of the coin with honesty, honor, and poverty. They show us what they want us to see, they tell us what they want us to know, and they tell us how we should feel about what we have seen and heard. Their strategy is to work top to bottom or inside out, distracting us from their hidden agenda.

They have us complaining when Republicans run the government, but have us feeling complacent when Democrats run it. Liberal thinking and policies have never worked in the pursuit to progress in life because they create dependency; and as long as there is dependency, someone stands to profit to the detriment of others. They have even made it seem that it is okay to be homeless, waiting for a politician or post-civil-rights community leader or activist to save the children and the elders. We say, "I don't care what nobody says; I love me some Al," or, "Wait, we have to give Obama time." But how long can we wait to receive nothing when our president would rather play golf than help the people who voted him in? Besides, if you understood politics, you would know that when a bill is signed by the president that "we the people" disagree with, it can take years to undo the damage. My hope is that "we the people" are not too loyal and too confused to accept the truth about Democrats. There are two types of politicians: one, which includes most of the Republicans, that stands for freedom and liberty for the American people; and the other, which includes the Democrats, that stands for segregation, poverty, and the spread of slavery internationally. Pick one.

No One Is Coming

During the 2008 presidential election, there were many Black Americans looking for instant help, but the president told them to "be patient and wait."[27] My guess is that the wait can be belittling. There is more to the Black American than begging for a handout. There is no one man who can define our destiny; and not all of us are waiting for a super hero to come and save us. Nevertheless, I bet there will be at least one leader in particular who will claim the

Black Agenda includes police brutality and will come to the rescue to save the president. Like it or not, if this president fails, the negative perception of Black Americans and our leaders will set us back more than we can imagine, thanks to President Obama. How long from now will it take for another Black American leader to be trusted enough to become the next Black president of the United States if we do not hold the first one accountable?

Change Your Thinking

We have to change our way of thinking. If we held a class teaching individuals how to find their God-given talents and purpose, the prison system and this party would vanish forever. Look at it this way: why is it that in many eyes the Democrats' voters are considered the poorest, most in need, in jail, and most likely less healthy? Unfortunately, we will depend on whom we think will help us the most. You have to understand, Black Americans cannot win if they are led by the Democrats. The Democratic Party does not care about the Democratic voters; no one in this Dependency Party wants you to better yourself. Now think about this strategy. Why do you think Al Sharpton, or as I call him, Dr. Revernstein, or any other leader that concurs with this agenda, would come on the radio every day and talk about racism, poverty, and President Obama, instead of about solutions and God? There is no solution to racism other than just to stop talking about it and start treating all people as you want to be treated. They know as long as you are afraid or confused you will need them. But the day you stop them from targeting you, that day racism will begin to die because you will have essentially destroyed the reason for their existence and voice. There is no one who can totally end racism because it is a personal problem implanted by a person's upbringing, and as long as it cannot be stopped, unless the individual chooses to change, the attitude will always surface. It is an individual right; it is a personal feeling toward another that keeps hatred going.

Absolutely no one can stop racism because it is a business for users and manipulators. It can stem from being dependent, being jealous, or not being informed. In fact, you cannot stop a person from hating you, but there are laws in place that will protect you from that person acting upon that hatred.

Image of Blacks

Marketing is a prime source of stimulating the economy. Poor people spend almost 100 percent of their earnings every year, more than any other group in America, but as a whole, they have no power. "Whoever controls the media controls the world." There is power for anyone in the withholding of the dollar. The media creates our perceptions of people, places, and things. The media makes most Black American females believe that most Black American males will not accept them unless they look like White women. In some cases, the media have helped others accept aspects of Black culture; the clothing, hair, jewelry, baggy pants, music, and slang are popular among White children. And a lot of White women love Black women's styles. In order for the world to change, the media will have to correct the negative image of Americans, especially among Black Americans. The media have purposely changed America by painting an image of the Black male as being crazy, mad, destructive, and the most feared human being on the planet. The media portray an illusion for you to think a certain way, again, to make you fear your own people, and to create hatred toward one another. This type of marketing has been very effective in selling an agenda, a product, a business, or an idea. This concept is a strategy that is a mental weapon; it programs the mind to favor an agenda for control and power. Leaders can use marketing to sell a brand or a product, provide a diversion, or create hype or fear in a certain marketed group of people. However, it has also been used to build trust or sympathy between two parties; but their job is to make you believe all of what they want you to see and all of what they want you to hear.

Marketing on the Gays

Even in today's society, this type of media promotes heterosexuals as being prejudiced, judgmental, and anti-gay when, in fact, the real issue is that no one wants to talk honestly about sexuality and racism. Most people who are affected, either because of their sexuality or their skin color, are constantly struggling to come to terms with their identity. They are hurting and struggling to find peace with self and God. As long as the majority of the media align themselves with the Democratic Party, they will do anything to keep the confusion going to promote their agenda. Anytime the Democratic Party physicians in the media know what is right but refuse to promote it in a godly way, it creates a diversion for a mass of people and creates dependency in them.

I have noticed how the media have marketed being gay as a new political party and the new popular Hollywood way of life. They use magazines, talk shows, and all other forms of media to promote new laws of acceptability. One of those laws teaches gay history in public schools. In a CNN article on July 14, 2011, it reported, "California governor signs bill requiring schools to teach gay history."[28] In that article with Democrat Governor Jerry Brown, it went on to say, "It will also require teachers to provide instruction on the role of people with disabilities." Again, this is why the Democrats cater to different groups—because, to them, they appear to have problems, be confused, or just need help. There are even psychologists and medical doctors that label this problem as gender identity disorder (GID). However, if being gay means being disabled or confused, why not offer some real help instead of promoting the gay lifestyle as glamorous on one day and a deficiency on another? How long will the Democrats use them before they decide to help them? My reason for speaking out on these matters is not to bash or belittle anyone but simply to shine light on our responsibility in being created in the image of God by helping those who are in need. What are the media so afraid of that they refuse to permit us to think for ourselves about these issues? From my research, I know so many of us claim some type of religious belief. In all of this research and data, I find it quite amazing that no dominant person or group will come out publically and discuss these issues. The Bible says to "love thy neighbor," and I will, but my only hope is that innocent children will not become fearful of God's plan for them or confused about their identity. The answer is to teach our children about God's laws on relationships, give them all of the facts, and then allow them the right to choose.

Historic Dismantlement in Order to Deceive

If you go back in history, you will see some of the same tactics used in the system of slavery. There were laws concerning slavery written as far back as the earliest days of the Babylonian Empire, long before the North and South ever had a conflict in America. In the period of 1700 BC, under the 282 laws in the Code of King Hammurabi, the founder of the Babylonian Empire, there were harsh punishments that were enforced such as, "An eye for an eye, a tooth for a tooth."[29, 30] For example, "Law 16: If a man has harbored in his house a male or female slave from a patrician's or plebeian's house, and has not caused the fugitive to leave on the demand of the officer over the slaves condemned to public forced labor, that householder shall be put to death."[31] Slavery consists of dependency and has been discovered in every ancient civilization, including ancient Rome, the ancient Egyptian culture, Akkadian Empire, Assyria, and ancient Greece, but the overall idea is free men versus slaves.

Slavery was a system of dependency that consisted of social stratification, the three-class model that included the rich, the middle class, and the poor. It created wealth, prestige, and power for some layers in a society on the backs of dependent slaves.[32, 33] Today, our society is separated into different groups of people according to their economic status, education, occupation, cultural organizations, and social groups. Some of these groups also associate with the larger national culture at times, but others stay separate, especially if they are the first or second generation removed from their country of origin. The slaves' masters, afraid of upheaval among the slaves, rewarded their informers among the slaves, planting the seed of distrust and confusion. By so doing, the masters were one step ahead of the slaves and any plans that they might have hatched against the system. Bear in mind that slavery was a system maintained by fear. The masters were afraid that the slaves might run away and they would lose their laborers, and the slaves were afraid of everything in general.

As I started to look into slavery around the early 1700s AD, on the banks of the James River, Virginia, in 1712, I stumbled over the tale of Willie Lynch, a Democratic provider, who stood in front of a crowd of plantation owners to present an idea on how to control their slaves without using violence. Willie Lynch's speech became a key method: "I use fear, distrust, and envy for control purposes," he stated in his speech. This lined up completely.

This strategy was to separate the slaves into many different categories. First was by age, by turning the young against the old and the old against the young. Second was by color, turning the lighter skinned Blacks against the darker skinned Blacks and the darker skinned Blacks against the lighter skinned Blacks. Then fine haired Blacks against coarse haired Blacks, tall Blacks against short, separating them by intelligence, size, sex, and anything that would be considered a difference. Lynch believed that, if a slave owner used this method, it would control the slaves for more than three hundred years to come.[34] Today, Lynch's methods continue to ignite fear in Blacks by using the Black leaders to control them—politicians, preachers, post-civil rights leaders, and others. They choose to separate them by status, the haves against the have-nots, the thinkers against the non-thinkers, the researchers against the non-researchers, and those who know the truth against those who do not. This Lynch method seems to have been adopted by the Democratic Party to create distrust and dependence so you will not gain faith, just the mindset of a slave. Walking in faith allows us to see the past as something to learn from and then release.

As I moved into researching the early 1900s, I found William Archibald Dunning, another contributing member that I call a "Democratic provider," the founder and president of the American Historical Association. Dependency and racism became a force that was placed upon Blacks. Dunning's idea was exactly the same mythology or methodology as the Democrats' as well: to restrict the publishing of certain highlights in Black American history by excluding these facts from history books and books in general. In a paper that he presented on December 29, 1913, at their annual conference for the American Historical Association, he stated, "It is best to make their history less interesting, at least they lived, they acted—they did things."[35] Dunning believed, "Black Americans were too inferior to hold political position." This caused a great amount of concern for W. E. B. Du Bois who often criticized and debated Dunning for his remarks and influence, including his support for the Confederate Army and the KKK, the providers and physicians of the Democratic Party's terrorist squad during the Civil Rights Movement.[36]

Image of Democrats

The Democratic Party between the years of 1865 and 1870 formed their first terrorist group, which many of you know today as the KKK, or the Ku Klux Klan, led by Nathan Bedford Forrest, the National Grand Wizard, a slave trader, and Confederate general. He is known for his comment, "That's a good thing; that's a damn good thing. We can use that to keep the niggers in their place."[37, 38] The Democrats used their supremacy organization to kill many innocent Blacks and terrorize them by instilling fear and hatred so that they would not vote unless they were voting Democrat; however, along with the many killings of Blacks, they also killed the Whites who were trying to help and protect the freedom of Blacks. We cannot forget the last known Klansman in the Democratic Party, Senator Robert Byrd, who died in 2010 at the age of ninety-two, the longest serving lawmaker in Congress; he served in the US House of Representatives for six years from 1953 until 1959 and as a US Senator for fifty-one years from 1959 to 2010.[39] In a 2010 column of the *Politics Daily*, Mary C. Curtis, a national correspondent, wrote "Byrd stated ambition made him do it." A smart move up from someone without connections."[40] Remember, Byrd voted against the 1964 Civil Rights Act.

The Klan has been playing the game very well by planting themselves in the Democratic Party. They cannot be trusted because they have always tried some type of scheme to fool the people. It used to be that Blacks picked cotton for them, but now all we have to do is just vote Democrat. The list goes on and on. Democrats have a habit of using fear to control our minds in order to make us dependent and afraid of trying. As long as our conscious minds judge our own efforts as weak, we cannot elevate ourselves. The Democratic Party is known as the anti-Blacks and slavery party; they are known for their tricks. They own most of the media, and they have recreated themselves to trick us into continuing to depend on them. However, we must be mindful and aware; many of them like to make promises, build us up with hope, and make us believe things will change if we hurry up and just wait on them.

The Obvious

On August 28, 2010, in Washington, DC, there came to pass two rallies celebrating Dr. King's commemorative speech, "I Have a Dream." Dr. Revernstein held the "Reclaiming the Dream" rally, and Glenn Beck, the "Restoring Honor" rally.[41, 42] Both men know how to draw a crowd, but for one of them, it was nothing more than a competition to see who could draw the biggest one. Beck drew about five hundred thousand people on the Mall of Washington and raised over five million dollars for the military's Special Forces families, and Sharpton drew about ten thousand people. It seemed that the only objective of Sharpton's group was to shout out racism and disrupt Glenn Beck's rally instead of focusing on the "Dream." Beck invited Sharpton to join them, but he refused. Did not Dr. King want all of us to stand together as one? Since Beck had the biggest venue because he scheduled the date first, would it not have made more sense to unite their groups? Beck's audience saw him as honorable with integrity, but Sharpton made Black Americans look embarrassed. To think after forty years we still cannot come together. For weeks, they used their radio and talk shows to market their events. Al Sharpton pulled the race card, but Glenn Beck had a more spiritual agenda that dealt with the rebuilding of the "Dream" of Dr. King. Even Alveda King, Dr. King's niece attended Beck's event along with other blacks around the world. What we must understand about marketing is that it is primarily about competing, and in every competition, someone has to lose. However, in this case, the one that plans well will always win. Dr. King's speech was over forty years ago, and his main purpose was unity, equal rights, and justice for all Americans to come together. On that day on the Washington Mall, most people did not realize that Dr. King had challenged the government to change; but look at that change now. We are still looking for it from another Black American, but where is it? When Black Americans rank the worst in every category and we are still proud to be Democrats, count me out. This Democratic Party is not working for me, and I am sure it did not work for Dr. King. "We the people" cannot afford to get caught up in the color of a person's skin for our livelihood and the futures of our own families. God says, "Love thy neighbor," and King said in his "I Have a Dream" speech: "I have a dream that one day, down in Alabama, with its vicious racists, with its governor having his lips dripping with the words of interposition and nullification; one day right there in Alabama, little black boys and black girls will be able to join hands with little white boys and white girls as sisters and brothers." If you have not improved your life or found prosperity in the Dream, when will you, because the only way you will see progress is when you embrace God's plan and King's Dream with work and the love for others.

Our Image for Our Children

Our children cannot wait. They are depending on us to stand up and make a difference. I want my sons to see me working, as one who takes advantage of opportunities, who takes calculated risks, and who is willing to knock down barriers. My boys should never see me weak because the food on my table comes from the money I earned honestly; and as long as I can work, we will eat. It is important to me for my sons to see me as an entrepreneur instead of someone else's lifelong employee. A man that sees the world as a business can measure the world in his hand, but a man that plans his world through someone else's business can only be measured in the hand of that man; no one gets rich on a job being controlled by others. When we as Black Americans can start to care for one another and care about how we are promoted in life and in the media, then we can change the perceptions of our past and of the Black American males. The real change starts when we can stop making excuses for not taking responsibility for our actions and our children. We must teach our boys the importance of being a man and how to look like businessmen instead of prisoners. Many of us have children and young siblings; many of us are too smart and too faithful to allow our image of ourselves to continue to be painted negatively. We seem to have lost our values. Not too long ago, the father and his son would make sure the daughter did not bring home the wrong fellow. They would lay down the law and the responsibilities of dating their daughter or sister, and if the fellow got out of line, he would have to deal with the consequences from her father or brother who would tell him how to treat her properly. But now, since the Democratic Destroyers of the economy and family are changing people, Americans are having to do whatever it takes to survive to feed themselves and their families, even if it means the devaluing of their image or the sellout of their worth. Understand this experiment is all in the effort to sell us dependency. This must stop.

Positive Images

This setup has made many believe that there are not a lot of successful Black Americans unless they are in sports or entertainment. But a good percentage of them are more than just that; they are business owners, doctors, lawyers, scientists, engineers, designers, inventors, mothers, and fathers, just to name a few. Under the Democratic leadership, we have not advanced the community or highlighted any successful images of us, just deadbeat dads and lazy individuals. As loyal as we are, they never tell us how to physically get out of our problem or even physically show us how to start the process, not to mention our own business. They are in the media more than anyone to change the perception of themselves, but they will not help their people.

God's plan for all of us is to grow and gain confidence, wisdom, knowledge, and understanding to prosper and help others. He wants us to create a better world for ourselves and our families, a world that we can be proud of and one that shows progress and prosperity. Let us start now by talking with our children and teaching them how to run a business. Let them know the new odds and challenges of becoming a good politician or president of the United States. This will show them not only that they can be great but also that they can be president of their own company. We cannot continue to let false leaders market us in the media as a party that likes to depend on others because the real agenda is the "Dream" and to obtain it "by any means necessary." We must re-create, re-invent, and re-establish our culture and our nationalism to build a new campaign with new leaders with fresh ideas. As a parent, you must teach marketing at home to your children so they will understand how it works, recognize when they are being targeted, and know how to resist it, and how to run a business or a campaign. Teach them how to create an idea, start a business, and market it to those who need it the most without taking freedom and dignity away from them. Also, make sure their marketing plan is laid out in detail for the time needed, whether it is for a course of months or years, before they inform others about their ideas, beliefs, and purpose. Make sure they do the research to think and learn their marketing target, and make sure they never fear their ability to succeed. They should know that a campaign is just a plan used every day to promote products and services, and an agenda to create fear in the minds of the majority. Teach them never to buy into using fear for marketing but understand its effects and consequences so they can protect themselves from Hollywood and the media that are controlled by the Democratic Party.

DIAGNOSING THE COMA

10

Our Faith: Ignoring the Evidence

Faith is the confident belief in a person or thing without having seen the person or thing.

So God created man in his own image, in the image of God he created him; male and female he created them.

—Genesis 1:27

After all the research and investigating the many problems, I never thought that praying for the Democratic Party would be the same as praying for poverty; and I never thought that praying for leaders would be the same as praying for liars. But since I was hooked and blinded in the Democratic Coma, I became capable of almost anything.

Our lack of knowledge has caused us to ignore the evidence of what the Democratic Party is about. Our faith in the party has taken away our ability to grow and find our true purpose and value. Because of that, we have become true victims of the schemes and plans of these people. The Democratic Party continues to eat up our praise and worship while they continue to play God, telling us what they think is good for us. As long as we keep praising them, they will keep playing God. We worship them as if they were heaven-sent to save us from the effects of slavery, but in fact, we have become enslaved by our blind loyalty to a group of undeserving people. We accept everything they offer, including the demeaning of our lives, misleading of our youths, and dismantling of our confidence in our God and in ourselves. In summary, they have convinced us that we cannot live without them.

The party's number one aim is to have us continue in this state of dependency and despair so we will not fight for change but be content in the Coma. The Democratic Party has managed over the years with strategic planning to strip us of self-worth and purpose. We have become totally dependent, weak, and without cause or purpose in our lives. We have allowed them to do whatever they feel like to us, and they take no thought of the consequences, for they have never had to answer to anyone. Their words are worthless because there is no sense of commitment to us or to God; there is no one that they believe they should have to answer to. They have become their own God; they are never wrong. In the meantime, we accept all that they offer us as truth. We lie unconscious, praying and doing nothing to pull away from the nightmare of the Democratic Party's Democratic Coma.

I, too, was hooked on the Democratic Party like a needle stuck in the arm of a junkie feening for a fix. They have us hooked on false hope, and we continue to pray and wait for them in blind unjustified faith, hoping for a fresh start that will never come. Many of us are left praying for heaven because we have given up on earth. We'll fight for the party, march for the party, and turn against each other for the party. I have even heard of some church people speaking in tongues and praying for the benefit of the party.[1] Some people would give their lives for the party as long as their candidate remains within the party. I, too, continued to remain in faith that the Democratic Party would come around for me. In the meantime, I was going broke. I lost 60 percent of my earnings, my car was running with the engine light on, and my "fixed" mortgage rate kept rising. All of this was because we put too much trust in the Democratic Party.

Most people will not admit that they are hooked because they are too embarrassed to look carefully at the facts, not knowing that all of this was designed by false leaders. In order to become unhooked, one must be willing to read, compare information, and have courage to be true to one's self. A man would be amazed at what he can do when he takes the time to sit down and just read. Blind faith is reserved for the deserving and proven. The question then is, what has the Democratic Party done for its voters to deserve this kind of loyalty? When tested, have they proven to be men and women of character, or do they always have an excuse ready for every apparent shortcoming? These questions are simple when put to the normal mind; however, when these simple questions are placed before an overzealous supporter, then it becomes almost impossible to get an honest answer.

Most people, in order to avoid the kind of introspection required to answer these questions, resort to the head-in-the-sand syndrome. Some people turn to religion and pray for death because heaven would be a welcome escape. Since so many of us believe in the party as if it was a god, the sense of helplessness is now so intense and the pain so very real that the human mind cannot handle it, and the questions are left unanswered. It has become too painful to question the obvious. This makes a difficult matter more difficult, seeing that ignoring the matter does not make it go away; it just prolongs it.

Never-ending Cycle

This kind of dependency is a vicious cycle that, if not stopped, will result in the destruction of America as we know it. We see it happening in Europe already. Because there is so much hurt and emotional pain involved in this matter, few politicians are willing to jeopardize their careers for the good of the people. This kind of dependency opens the door for abuse from the Democratic Party. Its leaders are skillful in dishing it out, continuing to manipulate us to their advantage. A great number of poor Democratic voters depend on and identify so closely with the party that, when the party fails, they see themselves as failing and then fall into a greater sense of dependency and despair.

The mind must have a focus. It was created that way and will find a point of focus whether that point is good or bad. The party will feed anyone who is willing to listen to their rhetoric full of discouragement, fear, and racism. They present themselves as kind and liberal, but they are infecting our minds with past disappointments and failures. When this kind of sad past is constantly preached, it wraps itself like a noose around the neck of anyone who is unfortunate enough to hear it. For the Black person, it creates anger, and anger without a constructive outlet produces violence. For the liberal White, it creates guilt and pity for the presumed victim instead of cultivating respect, trust, and equality. Blacks are no longer dumb slaves on the plantation; we are the equal of every man and woman regardless of race, color, or religion. White people do not need to be given a case of guilt; they need to be educated on who Blacks are and their value to this country, both then and now. To continue taking care of some Black Americans as if they were children is both unfair and unkind. It is no wonder some Whites resent us and consider us to be a burden. This country is known for its giving, and everyone needs help sometimes. However, it is better to teach a man to fish than always to give him a fish.[2] Help us to be all that we can be and do not prevent us. We, too, want to contribute to this country that is our country as much as any other US citizen's.

A sense of hopelessness and fear most often expresses itself in a destructive way. For example, we fight among ourselves or against anyone who opposes our way of thinking. I guess we fight among ourselves because we really do not have anyone else to fight with since most people do not want to live in our neighborhoods. Many people do not find our neighborhoods attractive because, not only do we fight each other, raising the crime rate, but also our neighborhoods have little or no public services. In essence, many Blacks live in the hood without any hope of ever leaving. The Democratic Party would have us believe there is no hope for our lives: we should be patient and wait for them to lead us to the Promised Land. This way of thinking encourages dependency and laziness. How long can we keep holding on when the trust given has not produced the anticipated result? After years of waiting and hoping, the feeling of loss intensifies, and anger emerges and presents itself as a solution to the problem. During that period of anger, sometimes crimes are committed, which results in further despair and hopelessness. The cycle goes on and on, but each time around is worse than the last. At the end of the day, there is not strength left to question why things are the way they are. Those of us that still have God as our hope continue to pray and wait but remain uninformed, still not knowing what to do because we refuse to read.

How Do You Question God?

In an article of September 25, 2011, by Zeke Miller in the *Business Insiders*, I read President Obama's words, saying, "Don't compare me to the Almighty; compare me to the alternative."[3] If we are told not to compare him with God why should we compare him with the Devil? Of what comparison and mindset should we measure him if he is not to be compared with God, yet the Devil is against all that God has created? So let's think, if the devil was asked to hang out with George Soros to destroy the America dollar, would he hang with him? Yes. But God wouldn't. If the devil was asked to hang out with Bill Ayers and other terrorists that want to destroy America, would he hang out with them? Yes. But God wouldn't. Now let's play Devil's advocate. If the Devil was told in order to control you he must trick Adam and Eve, would the devil trick them, curse you, and all generation after you? Yes, and he did but God did not! So if the Devil is a lie and still we are told not to compare the president to the truth, then what does this make our president?

How can a man with so much power and so much support want us to compare him with the Devil? When holding such a high rank that prevails over all, that is not what one should do. With so much excitement of having a fresh face, the possibility could make it hard for many to resist, but like any new face in any of our lives, we must question its existence. We question our children's friends, hoping they choose the right friends to surround themselves with. We compile tons of questions for the new teachers at the beginning of the year, because they have an eight-hour influence over our children's lives to shape their future. Even as parents, many of us are questioned by our own children when we cannot make it to their dearest events. So why not question this president when he holds the key to all of our futures? Now if being the president means we can question his action, when should we expect his image to reflect God? If he ranks next in command after God, holds the highest power on the land, and controls the world's deadliest weapon on earth at the sound of his voice, which image should we hope he possesses at a time of war if we cannot compare him with our God? Why not question him? If any alternative thinks that it can win over God and if his followers accept it as such, and this so-called alternative fails, then to what place shall the unfaithful be sent? Remember the old Negro spirituals our forefathers used to sing, songs with hope and promise of the redemptive power of a good God, one who will never fail us, a God that always cares. But if that God is replaced with a god that is put together by the Democratic Party, then hope is indeed lost. Unlike the God that our forefathers sang to and worshipped, the God that helped them to live and survive slavery is now replaced with a god that permits the government to run the household and remove the father as the head just to create confusion. Men like Al Sharpton, Jesse Jackson, Cornell West, Van Jones, and other poor leaders are given to us in place of a good source of education and an understanding of the value of self.

How can people reconcile with themselves when they have come to believe that they are failing and cannot stop themselves because they have given away their control? How does one regain control when the very tools that are necessary for a person to grow are not available to that person? Some supporters are so emotionally hurt and misguided that, in their attempt to fix the problem, turn to crime and violence, fighting against all odds, hoping against hope to find that germ of truth. When faith is misplaced, hopelessness and despair take hold. That sense of hopelessness will squeeze the life out of a person.

The cycle has again rotated as some Blacks seek jobs that cannot be found. Sometimes there are jobs, but in some cases, the applicants are not qualified socially and academically. It becomes especially hard on some young single Black mothers who are trying to support their children on food stamps, while they can hardly read or write. This is then further magnified because the companies that would normally hire are being killed off with higher taxes. The uneducated with children are more likely to raise children that will also be uneducated, and the circle continues to grow. The party's solution is more food stamps, welfare vouchers, underpayment of good teachers, and support of the unions that reward poor performance by giving poor teachers tenure. This serves the party very well because, by doing so, the party will always have someone to depend on them and thus vote them into office. This is an easier solution than insisting on higher educational standards and/or modifying welfare programs. To do this, they may lose votes, and the average politician would commit murder before losing a potential vote.

Misplaced Faith

The object of our faith must be worthy of that trust, for if the object of that faith is undeserving, the consequences could be devastating. It would be better to be faithless than to have misplaced faith. The object of your faith must be investigated and proven. Now, God is deserving of your faith. However, due to their lack of knowledge about God and His character, most people fail to rely on Him as their helper. This country was built on the reality of God and His faithfulness, and to date, He has not failed to be faithful. Most people fear the unknown. There is a remedy for that fear. However to acquire the antidote, the remedy must be sought with determination and honesty. The antidote is knowledge. Knowledge must be sought after with passion. Edison did not just stumble on the idea of the electric light bulb. He spent hours in his lab, and he sought the idea with his whole heart. And when the work-load became too overwhelming for him, he went looking for help and found Lewis Howard Latimer, an Africa-American who was self-taught in electricity. Latimer was also a patent specialist, and an inventor who developed and improved the carbon filament for those light bulbs to last longer and more cheaply. His first invention was the mechanical rail-road train toilet. The idea here is if you work hard you later reap the benefit.

The matter is made worse by those that claim to know about God, but have failed to teach the truth about Him or His ways. All people have the need to feel secure, and security comes with believing in someone other than the self. The drive to believe is strong because it encourages hope and a sense of belonging. The bad news is that if one fails to believe in the only person that will never mislead or misguide one, then all other reliance is going to be proven unreliable.

God is faithful, yet His faithfulness is forgotten by many. For example, God was good to Black Americans during the time when we were forced to sit in the back of buses and lynching was a weekly occurrence. Most Blacks had the understanding that God is good and will redeem. Today, God is no longer the center of our hope, and too often, His goodness is ignored. Then there is another group that just gives up on God altogether and replaces Him with the party and material things. There is yet another group that does just enough believing, hoping to gain enough points to get into heaven by faking faith. This last group is almost funny because trying to trick God is like trying to avoid death. God cannot be tricked since He already knows what the future holds and He knows all our thoughts.

There is another extreme among humans who profess to know God, those who do nothing but pray. Praying is not all we have; trying is all we have left. Faith requires action. God calls us to develop the talents He gave us and to use them to serve Him by helping our fellow man. A large part of praying is listening quietly to God's instructions for us for that day. Praying is necessary. However, due to lack of knowledge about God and about ourselves, many wait on God to do what they should be doing for themselves. Without faith, it is impossible to please God. Praying is great. However, it is working within the wisdom of God that makes it possible for all of us to succeed. When you fail to learn about a person's character, it becomes easier to be misled by false statements about that person because your confidence has not been rooted in knowledge. The object of this lesson is to know and understand the object of your faith.

God is the only One in whom you can truly trust with all your heart, mind, body, and soul, and not be disappointed. When you place your trust in anyone or anything other than God, constant disappointment will be the result. If trusting in God is not in first place in your life, all other relationships will suffer; it is God that supplies us with unconditional love that, in turn, enables us to love ourselves and one another.

In 2010, I noticed how the Democrats were starting to remove and attack God's purpose for America again. A US district judge of western Wisconsin, Barbara Crabb, who was nominated by Democrat President Jimmy Carter in 1979, ruled that the annual National Day of Prayer was unconstitutional, saying, "It violates the First Amendment establishment clause." Later in that same year, the Obama administration cancelled the annual ecumenical service at the White House, a tradition that had been practiced since 1954.[4] The idea here is to look at the character and the action of both parties to see their intent. In August of 2011, I found out why the president refuses to host the National Day of Prayer that was held at the White House by all former presidents. Instead, he stated, "Times like this remind us of the lesson of all great faiths, including Islam—that we do unto others as we would have them do unto us." On that same day, the president announced he would host the Iftar dinner in honor of Ramadan, "the ninth month of the Islamic calendar that consists of fasting that lasts 29 or 30 days."[5] This is the reason many think the president is anti-American. Remember, the Democrats have also challenged our faith by manufacturing lies to keep us in fear. David Barton, the founder and president of WallBuilders, a national pro-family organization, found other evidence that supports this theory. In an article on March 8, 2012, Barton stated, "President Obama is the most biblically-hostile US President," and he backs it well with many documents and footnotes.[6] You see, the Democrats feed us with distorted information to make us think the Republicans are the enemies. We must stop accepting the lies that we are fed and find the truth out for ourselves. They will continue to promote and challenge our faith and twist historical facts into confusion so we will not pursue our dreams. In fact, they do not want us to know who Dr. King Jr. and our ancestors were fighting against in the sixties or what party and people in government and the Congress were trying to block the Civil Rights Movement from being successful.

These things add to the strain, and the fear increases because we are not able to readily discern the cause of our failure. Many who call themselves Christian continue to pray only, not understanding their role as Christians. Prayer is good. However, praying without faith is useless, and where there is faith, there is progress. Faith is not docile; faith encourages growth, confidence, and godly self-esteem. Fear grows strong where there is no knowledge. Racism is passed down to our Black leaders who, in turn, pass it on to their followers and voters. The bitterness of racism has starved the average Black person of the will to learn and to prosper. All these things have contributed to the creation of poverty and the destruction of the Black family.

Some Clues Found in History

If you look at history, you will know there were many people that tested our faith by imposing themselves on the weak and the poor. They could take advantage of us because we lacked the knowledge of history, of what they had done before, of what others like them could do, all of which would have warned us to avoid them. Remember in the letter written by Willie Lynch, he described his method of training slaves to the benefit of his business.[7] One of those methods was creating confusion to use as a catalyst to increase production. What about the marketing of William Archibald Dunning and his scheme to change American history? Today these methods still exist in the Democratic Party. After the Civil Rights Movement, some leaders adapted ideas from Lynch's method of separating slaves based on their differences and from Dunning's idea of dividing people by characteristics and common sense. There are so many different religions that separate us, based on our beliefs. There are so many dependency-teaching pastors that target women to get to the men because if the pastors can draw the man they have the attention of the entire house. There are politicians that separate us by targeting our stands on dependence versus independence or freedom versus slavery, not to mention rich versus poor. If a man makes money, he should be entitled to keep it; giving should be voluntary, not forced. However, the best choice is to choose the leader that will not hinder your growth and then make that leader fight to keep your vote. Too many leaders will tell you one thing but do another just to create a distraction—as they have done with issues like abortion and contraception.

There are those whose very existence depends on the party. So when the party fails, they also see themselves as failures. As with the party, if your support comes from others, then you are not self-sufficient. Poverty, dependency, and racism continue to keep you in need. These things are still able to control us because we have not been taught faith correctly. Most people hold onto faith in man because they are afraid of trying anything else. In God's eyes, a person of faith should seek to find wisdom and understanding to prosper. The lack of faith and hope has weakened us. Some that proclaim faith and hope have no idea what true faith and hope are. Most of us use an unrealistic faith to procrastinate and avoid facing the truth. This gives a person with false faith the excuse needed to remain poor and sick. This allows one to sit around claiming hope, faith, and suffrage while starving.

Although we have been taught not to believe in ourselves, there is no excuse to continue in that vein. If one stops long enough to be honest with one's self, there is a need to find the truth; it will propel one to seek wisdom, knowledge, and understanding. The process of fulfilling one's dream starts with seeking the answers to the whys in one's life. God has done all that is needed for us to succeed. Reading and seeking will lead to understanding. Having faith in God is the beginning of wisdom, including of self. If you have no faith in God, you have no faith in yourself. Your faith in God is the foundation of your confidence, ambition, adaptability, and clear thinking. Faith in God is confidence in the relationship with God because of His character. God is loyal, loving, and committed. Knowledge and understanding of the object of your faith will enhance your confidence so fear will not be able to control you. However, where there is lack of knowledge, fear breeds.

Walking in faith allows us to see the past as something to learn from, and then we are able to move on to the next thing to overcome. After the assassination of Lincoln in 1865, most Blacks had faith until the Democratic President Andrew Johnson turned against Lincoln's Reconstruction

Plan by removing the protection of the US Army from within the Confederate States. One of the main purposes for the army's presence was to protect the slaves.[8] After this, the Confederate and the White supremacy groups went into high gear, imposing terror in free Blacks in an effort to keep them from voting. Most ex-slaves had great hopes and dreams that were destroyed soon after emancipation due to the beating given to them by the policies and rhetoric of the Democratic Party. They endured fear, racism, and dependency. Today many Blacks are still reliving that experience of the Reconstruction Era.

This country was founded on faith and on individual determination. In World Wars I and II, many of the Germans rejected the Bible and embraced a preacher who said that the Bible was not true, that Jesus was not God, and that they should believe in their conscience and not God to guide them. At the same time, America and her Allies believed strongly in their faith. Kaiser Wilhelm, the ruler of Germany in 1914, wanted the Germans to take over more land and access to the sea, so the Germans partnered with Austria-Hungary to fight against Serbia. Then Russia promised to help Serbia, and France promised to help Russia. This made the Germans angry, they declared war on France, and then both allies were fighting each other. Up until March of 1917, the Germans had promised Mexico a part of the United States, hoping that America would not find out; but they did. President Woodrow Wilson became angry, joined the Allies, and declared war on Germany. Because of the German's lack of faith, on November 11, 1918, the Germans and all of their allies surrendered, and World War I ended, with America and her allies standing strong in victory.[9] In life, we must embrace faith and believe in the existence of God. Although the Germans fought, kept trying, and gave a good fight, their faith was not strong enough to stand up to the Americans and their allies.

Looking over Self

It is because of misguided faith that we do not trust who we are and we deny our responsibility and independence. It is because of our history, our choosing dependence, and our choosing fear that we lost our confidence and purpose in life. Since we do not trust ourselves, we do not trust God. We have changed the destiny and purpose of our lives. A man's biggest fear is of self; he must first trust himself before he can trust in others. It is that same fear that has been extended to each other that has made many of us spread our virus of ignorance to others. Many Blacks refuse to use Black doctors and Black attorneys, but they are quick to call it racism when it comes from another race. In addition, due to a lack of righteous faith, many spend their time trying to get over, get by, and/or be slick, getting themselves into further despair. Some spend so much time scheming on how they can con the government instead of preparing and perfecting their gifts.

I read about a person who borrowed a friend's child in order to get more money back in his tax refund. There were also two young college girls who chose to rob a bank instead of finishing school and living free. So many spend years trying to get by because they have set such very low standards for themselves. If you expect less, you receive less. There was a young woman that I knew who had five children by five different daddies. She was now pregnant with her sixth child by a sixth man. This guy was a sneak and a drunk. He had been arrested ninety-three times and was in a rehab center when they met. She had his baby, and then she started to complain that he needed to get a job. My question is where was her mind when she allowed this man to father her sixth child? In life, every decision must be weighed and evaluated because there are always consequences to one's choices.

Laziness

Same leaders use the Bible to further their agenda. In the Bible, God called leaders, wise men and prophets. Their duties included helping the needy and poor to find faith, wisdom, and knowledge.

God's word encourages our doing for others. Many leaders would have you focusing on the needs of others by marching and having prayer vigils when your families are in trouble. Many of us have gotten so caught up in the fascination of memorizing the Bible rather than seeking to understand it. We have lost our mojo, and have dropped the ball by allowing others to use our faith against us. Where does it state that we should sit down and do nothing? Tell me, where does it say that we should beg for the rest of our lives? Now tell me where it says that you cannot start your own business and be successful. Tell me where it says that you have to go around to the back to be served in a restaurant. Then tell me where it states that you cannot vote in America. Tell me where it says that you cannot integrate with White Americans in a free society with many opportunities. Tell me where it says that you cannot be the most powerful man or woman in the world, the president of the United States of America. We should dream for the future. But they want us to dream about the past and about racism. Instead of encouraging us, they instill fear; instead of our having freedom of choice, they shackle us in their Democratic Party.

Keeping Faith

I remember talking with a young woman who voted for the Democratic Party. I was providing her with life coaching when she told me how miserable her life had been and that many times she had contemplated committing suicide. This all started during her college years when she contracted an STD from an old boyfriend, who was also a Democratic voter. She said to me, "I guess this is the life that God wants me to have." I quickly replied, "You are in charge and in control of your life, not God. He has already done the work for you. He is the overseer and the witness to the many choices that we make."

In the beginning, God created life and gave everything in the world a purpose. Because this young woman had lost faith, she also had lost hope in herself to prosper. God has done the work. He will not make any decision for you; He is just a witness that monitors your faith through your many choices, triumphs, successes, failures, and consequences. He has given you all that is needed to be a success.

Since the beginning of time, the work of God has already been done for us to grow and prosper. For those who think that He will come down and show us the way, he has already shown it to us. He waits, monitoring our faith, expecting that one day we will recognize that we have all the tools needed to pursue our purpose and achieve our dreams. By now, you have gained the knowledge and understanding to recognize that it is now left up to you to make choices that will lead to success. You are given the vision and the ability to believe. You can do anything by faith in God and following His way of doing things. Trust in God and His teachings, and you will find the wisdom to believe in God's kind of faith.

We can learn from history and the wisdom of God found in the Bible. No one would be here except for the goodness of God. Since God is the creator, He knows the outcome, the process, the purpose, the future, and the capabilities of all things. As I ended my conversation with this young woman, I said to her, "God doesn't determine your life; you determine your life." God has already done the work, which makes Him knowledgeable about all the things in this world before and after they occur. He has the ability to see your answer, your response, your consequences, and your next move. Because God has already done the work, He now just witnesses our decisions and choices. He knows the outcome of our choices and decisions. He will not act for us; He will not choose for us. He will only watch over us, hoping that we remain faithful and respectful in choosing. We are spending so much time hoping, praying, and waiting for confirmation, not knowing that He is our confidence and confirmation to prosper. You have to believe and trust that God has paved the way before you can take the journey.

In other words, stop spending a lot of time waiting for God when He is waiting for you.

Take Responsibility

Because of my faith in God, I know I can be anything; I just never took the time to search and act out that theory. It was not until I was asked to speak at a church function to children that I recognized that faith in God was my confidence and, therefore, I could not fail. While searching for that right topic to speak on, I picked up a Bible; when I opened it, I found my answer in Genesis 3:26, "For the Lord shall be thy confidence and shall keep thy foot from being taken." What a very ironic situation. Never in my wildest dreams would I imagine that it could happen, but that moment gave me a strong sense of confirmation that I had found my talking points. You see, in order for anything to happen, you must first believe that it can and then apply the effort to make it a reality. Many of you think that your life is over or you do not have a purpose, but with faith in God and a little effort, success is just around the corner. At this point, you can no longer sit and hope that someone who is better off will be guiding you.

As I sit here and ponder on my life, I think about how my father and mother were misled and given the wrong information about faith, how they would have been better parents but, because of their lack of knowledge, they were unable to pass the truth down to my brother and sister and me. They sent us off to Sunday school, hoping that the pastor would lead us in the right direction. The truth was that the pastor himself did not know; he knew only how to teach praying because he never asked us to try. Later, when I got a little older, my uncle would come by the house to get my father to allow us to go with him to church so that we could be baptized, but for what reason, we did not know. My uncle thought it would help us get closer to God, but after two baptisms, we still did not know how to get close to God, and we still did not get our answer. I appealed to my uncle, but he did not know the answer himself. So, now I ask this question, "What is faith with no answer?" I think about all of the people in the neighborhood that watched over us when our parents were not at home. I do not know whether they knew the answer; all they could say was, "Stay out of trouble." I think about all the corner preachers that had something to say, but they did not know; they just kept repeating, "Jesus is coming back," or, "The end of the world is near." I think about how important history and science are today, how incorrectly it was taught to us in church and in school and, most important, who taught it to us. I reflected, "If all of us come from the same community, the same struggle, taught under the same failed curriculum, did the pastors and teachers really know, or were they playing dependency as well? Were they just faking?"

If they had just told us the purpose of the history book, I would have had more faith in understanding finances, marketing, my rights, and the Constitution twenty years ago. If they had told me more about my faith and purpose in science to understand my existence, I would have seen my gift was in inventing, producing, and creating a product earlier in my life. I would have tried. If they had told me how much I truly needed to understand language, this first book would be my tenth book. Nevertheless, if I had been told about God's purpose for me earlier, I would have led many of you out of this misguided depression that we have been enduring for decades. I even wish if they would have told me more about my history during the Civil War, the Reconstruction Era, and how God created me, then I would have shown you how to prosper earlier and achieved most of my goals by my eighteenth birthday. For many of us, I do not believe that faith is all there is; I believe that true faith requires works. If not for the wrong teaching, misguided information, and the confusing information about God, we could be prospering and enjoying our time on earth. So I tell all of you, find the truth; do not give up. Your family is depending on you.

Faith Pursues Its Desire

In 2004, my wife and I wanted to have another child, and she became pregnant. The doctor told her that if she had another child she could die, based on her diagnosed disease, called hyperemesis. However, if she had the baby, it might have Downs Syndrome or be deformed and missing some limbs. At that moment, she became scared, but she was willing to take the chance anyway. She realized she was no longer in control, but she was willing to die for her child. When you are not in control of a situation, fear is your biggest downfall. Hyperemesis is a pregnancy disorder that causes the organs to shut down, which results in excessive vomiting and damage to the liver, gallbladder, and kidney. The doctor told her that she had a 10 percent chance of living if she continued with the pregnancy. She would have to decide whose life was more important. The doctor said if it came down to it, he would have to save her life instead of the child's. She decided to have our child and that her life was not that important. This was a very frightening situation to be in, but I was convinced that, because my child was a gift from God, there would be nothing wrong with him. I refused to believe and accept that any child of mine would have anything wrong with him, and I refused to believe that my wife would lose her life in bearing this child. I called on God and said, "God I cannot accept this." A small voice spoke to me, and it said, "Then don't."

On March 26, 2005, my son was born as healthy as he could be. By the age of sixteen months, he was operating a computer better than any five-year-old. As of this writing, he is six years old and can operate that same computer better than most adults. Taking chances requires a little faith, patience, and intelligence because no one has all of the answers to the possibilities. Now is the time for all of us to understand the game and to teach our children confidence, self-esteem, and courage so they will have the faith to be able to become great in life. Faith and works go together.

We are made in the image of Christ, so why should I believe that humble is to think less of myself? Should I not show my love for Him in order to convince others that He is great and that we are made out of greatness? Psalm 82:6 says, "You are God, Son of the most high," and Exodus 3:14 says, "I am who I am." I am made in His image. If humble is to think less of yourself, then this would be a contradiction for lack of confidence keeps you from trying and applying efforts. Trying encourages growth and self-esteem, but when you are not aware, not prepared, or lack the knowledge of self and purpose, it creates fear. Why should we claim humble for it sends us back to fear? We should love God as we love ourselves; we must align our will with God's.

You see, if humble means to think less of yourself, then this means we should not be confident. Speaking about the greatness in me is not pride. Beauty and greatness were placed in me by a higher power. Recognizing the greatness that is placed in me is not pride. Pride fails to acknowledge that greatness of God in me and leans on the "kindness" of the politicians. If you have ever thought that you could not make it, would not the change come from within to have faith in God and yourself or belief that you can by using the Word that lives within you to try? You must start now, stop doubting yourself, and believe that God and the God in you will fulfill all of your needs. Faith is the answer, your faith is your confidence, and your faith is all you have to make a better life for you and your family. Do not let fear hold you back. Do not let your fear become your weakness. You cannot lose faith and hope, and you cannot rebound back for a second chance if you do not try. Failure is not accepted, and not trying is not an option. Faith is hope that keeps us going, and it is faith that gives us strength when we are weak. What are hope and faith if they do not come with an answer?

Faith comes from an old Latin word, *fidem,* or in other cases, *fidere,* a verb from 1200 BC that means to trust. Faith is like the verb, the action word, in a sentence; therefore faith and action go together. The purpose in your life is like the subject, what acts upon the verb. Subject and verb join together to make a complete sentence, and your purpose and your faith join together to make a complete life. Now, if we have no subject and no action, your faith is not growing. Faith needs a subject on which to focus its energy. Give your faith something to work on.

Even when acting, many have taken action for something or some other person and not themselves. Prosperity opens the mind to see many opportunities to grow. Faith encourages your beliefs to achieve them. This is one of the reasons many of you believe that you were born without action to prosper. But faith can be confused when it is taught because a person with no faith will depend on others and never prosper or possess independent growth without fear.

We are at the end now. What do we do? You cannot continue to remain silent while the Democrats destroy what is left of this country that gave man freedom. We must do something before it is too late. America's children need a guaranteed shot at a good life and not a life of dependency. Your vote is what you have left. Cast it. I HOPE this is not … the end …

CURING THE COMA

11

The Prescription

Truth

There is absolutely nothing that we cannot do when we know the truth and follow God's plans. Knowing truth is the prescription, the cure, and the antidote for having a truthful life. Truth is accurate, truth is real, and truth brings a halt to deception when it appears. Truth is consistent; it provides the level of integrity required of an honest man. When a man's character is developed in truth, his actions will reflect the sincerity of his heart. His actions will speak truth when he is honest; but if he does not recognize truth, or if he denies truth, the consequences become unbearable for him. Truth is pure and kind, and when it is sincere and honest, it is of God.

Truth does not give false hope; neither does it gives a partial picture. Truth gives the whole story, leaving nothing out. Truth is unchangeable; it is the only thing that we can believe in that is real. When there is truth, there is God's will. His truth lasts throughout any and all changes, forever and for all generations to come. It does not matter what color you are or how different you may be; if your character is not pure in truth, the content of your words and actions will be contaminated. Truth is the soul of freedom; it releases all doubt. It will never lead astray. God's truth is calm, patient, and always timeless.

Everything that is of substance is made of truth. Truth heals the sick, gives strength to the weak, and renews the soul of the soulless. There is nothing that we cannot do when we have the truth in our hearts. Even unbelievers will one day have to face the truth and pay a steep price if they want a clear vision of their destination. Truth is knowledge;

it prepares the unprepared. Truth will shine light to expose what is hidden in the dark. Truth is the only thing that is complete; it leaves a lying mouth closed after confrontation. In truth, there is love and hope that are everlasting. Truth is the confidence in one's journey that infuses hope through each trail. It clears the path to prevent stumbling.

Truth does not make mistakes. It is always on time and on purpose. It does not create chaos; it resolves chaos. Truth will never follow blindly but will acknowledge only that which is honest and pure. Truth is correct, it is flawless, and it does not make wrong choices. It analyzes, investigates, and provides facts for the benefit of the seeker. Truth is not always pleasant for the listener, and lying about the truth surely does not make it go away. Truth is light; it shows you what is right and wrong and then gives you the opportunity to make changes. It is never too late to practice truth. It is ready when you are. The idea is to take it one step at a time. Walk if you are not ready to run, and sit if you are not ready to walk. Truth will sit and wait with you if you are tired; truth will let you rest. Just know it is not too late because, when you are ready, He is waiting and would love to hear from you.

Start by reading a good book or just be kind to yourself. Take time to evaluate where you are in life and start making plans to get to the next point. In all of this, love yourself and keep on hoping and planning. It is never too late to plant the seed; just make sure it will last long after we are gone. Some people never live to see the results of what they have planted. Lincoln planted the seed of freeing the slaves but never lived to see the results for those who accepted it. Dr. King planted the seeds of love and equality but never got to see them accepted and fulfilled. Alexander Bell planted the seed of the telephone but never got the chance to see it actually work. So when you plant your seed, know you are not planting it just for you; you are planting it also for many generations that will come behind you. It will not matter where you come from or who you are. Be strong; there is nothing you cannot do when you know truth and focus on it. Remember, your labor will not be in vain because truth also provides immediate benefits.

Recognize Your Values

Who you are is not determined by what you have or, as Dr. King once said, "by the color of your skin but by the content of your character." What you have does not mean anything if it is not embedded in the truth. Some spend a lifetime attaching themselves to unworthy things, things that are poor substitutes for the truth. We are placed in this world to do great things that are honorable and just. Whether or not we do great things will depend on what we value. Our greatness can only be of value when others benefit from our actions. Find what is worthy of honor; then study it and respect it by imitating it.

Without principles that are honorable, the future of man will be lost. Whom we honor and imitate is also of great importance. We must evaluate both with all the honesty we can muster. Where there is no honor, there is failure. The prisons are full of people who were never taught to honor worthy people and worthy goals, so they live out the sad consequences of dishonorable lives. A man's actions reveal whom he has chosen to honor once his life is exposed for all to see, so it is important to choose wisely so others can remember the good in you.

If we have not carefully chosen worthy values to live by, we give the deceivers in this life an open season to hunt us down, misuse us, and destroy us. As long as we can be painfully honest with ourselves, truth will guide us wisely. No one can be fooled if he is aware of the foolishness and its consequences. What we focus on will define the path on which we travel. To lose sight of one's destiny and choose wrong values will leave us lost. Our values will determine our destiny; therefore, it is important to be awake to every decision we make. Living out worthy values will make it easy for others to recognize our goodwill. A kind heart and caring soul will clearly show their roots. We are all God's children, imbued with His love to accomplish great things as long as we follow His plan faithfully.

Nothing is worth having if it does not come from a firm foundation of true constructive values. America cannot survive if she refuses to stand with her founders on what has always made her great. After all, what other kind of source could there be than that of one's creator? Those things that are truly important and honorable will last a lifetime and beyond.

Poor Planning

No genuine success is accidental; it must be planned. With planning comes awareness and readiness to succeed. You do not need a plan to fail, but you do need a plan to succeed. Failure looks for those who are not ready or who have not prepared themselves. From the minute you are born, it looks for failure to which to attach itself. But with truth, its preparation will always repel failure and evil. With truth, there is no failure. There is no one who can force you to turn left when you know to turn right. In order to correct the problem, you must be aware of the problem. But you do not necessarily need to decide on a plan before working the problem; just do what you love, and success may come. A child writing in a journal may not be aware of his plan at first, but later he may find himself the author of a life-changing book. As long as you keep searching, you will find it. The idea is to take one day at a time and stay focused.

Be Courageous

David knew that Goliath was a giant, but David did not care because he trusted in God's help more than he feared his enemy. Having courage does not mean my encounter will not be difficult. It just means I will not stand for anything holding me back anymore because my problem will just get bigger if I wait till tomorrow. Truth gives strength to courage. When you know truth is in sight, your plan will last. Now I do not know about you, but as with David's battle with Goliath, I need that same amount of courage to stand on the things that I truly believe in.

There is nothing that we cannot do when our mind is focused on a worthy goal. There is something special about all of us—black, white, and brown. We are all human beings, born for greatness, created by the greatest Scientist and Creator of the universe to be the most important species on this planet. We are the only species that has so many unique capabilities and talents. We have the ability to change things to make them better, and we can do things just to show they can be done. All of us have a purpose; through God's love and strength, we are able to achieve it. The past is behind us; the truth stands out in front. It is here where we put away the blame game and see that this country is full of possibilities and opportunities for us. God loves us and wants us to succeed as long as we love ourselves and one another. He created us to succeed. Why do we hold ourselves back from succeeding? Why do we try to destroy our chances?

No longer should we let fear or false pride or ignorance lead us astray when there is truth right in front of us. Truth and knowledge are part of a creative life lived in God's love. Nothing exists that holds more possibilities for a creative life than truth. Truth, reality, creativity, love, and success are all part of God's plan for our lives. When you know it in your deepest self, you can become passionate about using your talents to create a happy and fulfilling life. Open yourself up to the possibilities that God gives us in this life and succeed in creating the best you, and help your family to do the same.

America is the greatest country in the world, built on the belief that man can do anything and be anything as long as he is willing to acquire the knowledge to put ideas into action. America is a country that was built to offer freedom to everyone who wants to realize a good life, and it is the place where I have received it. No other country has ever offered a person so much opportunity, but we have to beware of people who try to take our freedoms from us. With opportunity comes the responsibility to protect our freedoms. We have to be aware of the voices around us that are pulling us in different directions. God has given us life, talents, and potential. We must develop them to build a happy, fulfilling life for ourselves and our families.

THE REHAB

12

Four-step Recovery

1. Knowing Business: The Forgotten Profession

In order to cure ourselves of this Coma, we must first wake up and accept that we have been in a Coma. But to succeed, we must know and appreciate self; however, by doing so, we must also recognize our responsibilities, our business, our gifts, our weaknesses and learn the laws for how to achieve success for ourselves.

For many years, we have used our personal feelings to handle our business because we did not know business, finance, marketing, and history. We stopped building ourselves up. We stopped searching for our own direction and purpose. We stopped searching for meaning in our existence. And we even stopped contributing to the business within ourselves. Life is a business that we invest in; success comes from what we put into it. Each and every one of us was born with a "business," and like any business, it is expected to grow and prosper. Our "business" is in the way we act, the way we speak, the way we dress, the way we look, and how we feel toward ourselves and others. When we are not able to identify our selves, many of us end up lacking confidence.

In business, you learn to think, and you learn the principles of the business—how to create the business, market the business, operate the business, and enjoy all the benefits from investing in a successful business. Now, if we take that same approach with our personal feelings and create out of them a successful inner business, our lives will expand. The idea is to feed the mind with information that is relevant so that we can make better choices instead of spinning our wheels in a morass of unruly, confused personal feelings. When all things are done and all decisions are made after careful reasoning and deliberation, the truth is not easily discarded if others find it offensive.

In life, we make friends, and in business, we generate a clientele. These relationships can elevate us to the next level, but if our personal feelings are not controlled by a wise mind, our business will most likely fail. The goal is to treat people right by seeing them as potential customers or supporters. If we treat them with respect, there is the greatest chance they will come back and continue to support us. A negative, disrespectful attitude can break a deal and create all kinds of misery for ourselves. Business men and women do not care about excuses; what they care about most is what you have to offer them. It does not matter where you come from or what color you are; if you have something that they need, they will buy it or trade with you. Your appearance is another factor; it means everything. If you are the one selling or providing the service, you must look the part to get the part. The idea is to look as if you already have it in order to obtain it. No one wants to be caught doing business with someone that does not have some form of business ethics. If you want the greatest outcome, you give the greatest beginning.

Business is not personal; it is an economic system that consists of providing a service or a product. The more you provide or produce, the more you advance in those relationships. In business, it is not about you; it is about solving the problem through you. Your reputation is everything; it is the result of your work in dealing consistently with skeptics and believers alike. If your reputation is good, mark my word, you will see the pot of gold at the end of the rainbow.

What we have been taught but have failed to see is that every ethnic group that has come to America has had a plan for building a future, except for us who were forced to come. But now things are different. There is nothing holding us back. In order for us to change our future, we must create one and learn how business works in order to achieve our goal of a better life. Now, we can conduct business using only uncontrolled, personal feelings or by using informed, organized minds. It is our choice. To succeed, we must learn to put our emotions aside to see the big picture calmly and reasonably. What will we gain from an emotional transaction that gets too personal? If you follow a reasonable, realistic plan, you will learn to market your business, operate your business, and enjoy all the benefits of investing in a successful business.

"If it doesn't make money, it doesn't make sense." On whom should we place the fault if we approach a situation personally, letting our emotions affect our growth? Whatever you want is yours through your own hard work and sacrifice. In order for one to become successful, one must prepare to be successful by acquiring the knowhow, the mindset, and the right approach. We can operate our lives as a business, being professional and rational while positioning ourselves for growth, or we can continue to fail by acting foolishly and thinking someone owes us something. The business approach with a serious mindset is the one approach that prepares us to be self-sufficient and free. This allows us to market ourselves in a professional manner, treating others as decent human beings or as potential customers by our ethical behavior. Our personal business of being a reliable, trustworthy, self-respecting, and respectful Self is one in which we become the owner and the CEO of ourselves and our future. As for dreaming of a better life, it is an individual, private matter. We work to realize our own dreams, waiting for the time when our efforts toward a realistic goal will take their course and succeed. Only time will define the reality of our dream; dreams and visions that do not produce are a waste of thought.

It is part of our personal business to train our children's minds to be business-like, to think like a professional, and to provide them with the best education we can give them. This includes our at-home reinforcement of teaching them about history and the Constitution, exposing them to different cultures, and enrolling them into different, enriching off-campus programs. It is part of our responsibility to also stimulate their interest in science, math, and technology just so they will be exposed to everything. It is our job to teach them proper manners and how to treat others and communicate with them. If we succeed in our parental role, we will have made the best investment and created the best business ideas for them to succeed. This concept will become our legacy, our business plan, with all of us being the beneficiary, the manager, and the investor in this company of Self. Now, call it what you want and get emotional, but one thing is certain: we must keep our personal feelings out of it for our business to succeed because business is still business and prospering is the main goal. You can live your life in the hands of a businessman or be the businessman with others' in yours. Choose one.

As 1 Thessalonians 4:11–12 says, "Make it your goal to live a quiet life, minding your own business and working with your hands, just as we instructed you before, so that your daily life may win the respect of outsiders and so that you will not be dependent on anyone." Never depend on anyone but yourself; this is the way to do everything successfully using a business approach.

2. Knowing the Laws: Rules and Regulations

America is a nation of laws. Life itself is like a game. To know how to play and win at it, we must understand and study its rules and instructions. There are those that study the game, and there are those that do not. But make no mistake, there is absolutely no one that can succeed without studying them. Laws, rules, and instructions are the foundation for advancing. All of us, at every moment in our lives, must follow some set of principles or ethical system just to overcome the challenges in life and push beyond them to succeed. It is essential that we understand the foundation.

Whoever understands the rules and follows the directions within its system will advance to the next level.

No matter how many times we try to deny it, "the law is simply just the law," and there is no other way around it. The laws that we are supposed to abide by are made to protect us from others who would interfere with our progress and protect others from our interference with theirs. When you obey the laws, your ambitions and your confidence can progress. When your actions have not followed any principle, you will eventually fail, disrupting and damaging a lot of lives unnecessarily. If you are not prepared to stand and face the obstacles and challenges in life because you do not know right from wrong, you may lose your freedom forever. Someday after all laws have been made, after all games have been played, and after all options have been tried, all of us will have to believe in some type of principle, but it may be too late.

Laws of the Land

The only way to participate in changing a situation is to study it and learn what the situation requires. Most games played are political, and because they control the present and future of America, it is your responsibility to learn the law, including the Constitution, the Declaration of Independence, the Bill of Rights, and what the Founding Fathers intended when they wrote them. Whether you agree with them or not, they created the blueprint for how this country should operate and how it must protect its citizens so we can all grow, achieve prosperity, maintain good health, and pursue happiness. However, if the new ones that Obama and the Democrats are imposing on us can change America, it certainly can change you, your thoughts, and your dreams.

This country was founded on principles intended to protect our liberty, freedom, and religious beliefs as citizen of the United States as long as we abide by the laws. But in the event that we do not, we lose, and someone else profits from our laziness and ambitious mistakes. When we follow the rules, we flourish. Just like America as a nation, we are accountable for our own home. Our objective is to take responsibility for ourselves, just as it was intended that America depend on itself alone and not become indebted to any other nation, like our enemy China.

The Constitution is one of the most important legal documents that we must follow, along with the Ten Commandments in the Bible. Unfortunately, many of us have wasted too much time in scheming to get around these laws, only to find out that our rebellion has brought on terrible consequences for ourselves. Since many of us cannot accept America as home, many of us have struggled unnecessarily harder than others. We must learn these laws and understand their worth and purpose to preserve the legacy of our freedoms and responsibilities.

Our legacy involves knowing that this country was built on laws and rules that protect the rights of its citizens. The first plan of laws was called the Articles of Confederation, which gave the states their freedom and independence over an intrusive national government. But they lacked an executive agency or president, a way to tax the people to provide for a military, and a way to pay off a national debt in case any enemy attacked us. It took until 1787 to put the first laws in place, the Constitution of the United States. In 1787, our Founding Fathers met in Philadelphia at the Constitutional Convention to sign the Declaration of Independence, based on the Bible and our God-given rights. These laws became the blueprint that outlined the behavior and freedoms of an American people independent of any oppressive government or any outside government. Since those laws were ratified, they have become the instructions for how this country should function.

It was at those moments that the Founding Fathers wrote the playbook for America, the laws of the land. By knowing and abiding by them, we all reap the greatest benefits by prospering and remaining free. These laws were made to protect our freedoms and our religions from being imposed upon by our government or anyone that would interfere with our growth, foreign or domestic.

When you get a good understanding of America's laws and history, then you can change your life. America is your home. Learn how to live in it. We have to let those who want to fight certain battles fight, but in the meantime, you must move forward with a better agenda, to feed and protect your family by using the laws of the country. The methods or complaints that you have heard from the Black leaders about the advancement of Black Americans thus far have not worked; but the philosophy of other cultures has worked for them because they chose to follow some set of rules. You see, having the key to a locked door is much better than kicking down a door with no key. The idea is to be prepared and follow the rules that will align you with succeeding.

A man's most valuable assets are his gift, his family, and his knowledge, which he can pass down to his children and his children's children. In today's society, your children are the key to your legacy and your journey to create a wealthy future. Teach them the laws of this country and protect them with everything you have because as long as you are not aware of some needed information, there will always be problems. The less you know, the more lavish these Democratic physicians' lives get.

When we were in school, we took so many of the subjects for granted, mainly because we thought they served no purpose or were not important. But lately, they have come to be very important. Now we are in a state of emergency, and we must take history and the laws seriously in order to grow. We must learn the laws to avoid the consequences of breaking them. A man's greatest asset is knowledge, and the more he learns, the more he prospers. This plan is very simple. If man does not play to win, how can man eat?

Not Knowing the Simple Principle

Everything in life has some type of system in which it operates that determines its growth, existence, and success. By gaining wisdom, knowledge, and understanding of these systems, structures, and principles, we gain the keys to achieving success. When we follow these laws, we choose the most valuable path for a quality existence and future.

The future is controlled by many systems that create order by governing man's behavior. A system of laws helps us formulate strong moral standards and values. These laws protect our passage through different phases to reach our goals; but when we lack the knowledge for how to achieve them, we fail. The solution lies in learning the system of laws to play in the game of life.

Many of us do not know the rules for playing the game, but if we want to win, we will learn them, follow them, and win. Gaining this knowledge gives us plenty of room to grow and flourish and reach the next stage. One of the basic rules ordains that if we accept responsibility to work hard and obey the laws, we will make a better life for ourselves and our family. In our lives, we will always have rules—in the legal system, the financial system, the political system, etc.—that guide us in finding better outcomes. The basic principle is as simple for you as it is for any American: you have to learn the rules to the game to win.

3. Knowing Your Strength

Everyone has a weakness, but all of us also have the strength to change our lives. In order to make that transition, we must be able to recognize the difference between the two. Time and research have proven that to know your history is to find your strength in your purpose. History consists of people's experiences and events that have occurred. There are those who have suffered from their weaknesses, and there are those who have achieved a certain amount of success. Using our strength is the only answer. Knowing history creates a strong level of growth and understanding so we can avoid making the same mistakes of the past in similar situations of today.

There will be many obstacles and barriers in each of our lives. Reading the diaries and letters of how our ancestors handled their troubles helps us understand that we are not alone in any difficulty. We realize others have gone through similar problems and survived and were the better for it. It is up to us to find that strength and courage we need to discover our dreams and purpose. Every moment we waste postpones our fulfillment. Without strength and belief and effort, we fail to see our imagination turn into reality. We have faced so many setbacks and so many consequences from our wrong choices that we have lost sight of our future. Our poor choices, our confusion, and our disillusionment have caused us to picture life as hopeless. But we can elevate ourselves by continuing to grow and learn about ourselves and others. In life, there is a process of growth. Either we choose to lose ourselves to all hope, moving downward toward death, or we choose to be a creative part of life, moving upward in hope.

Imagine everything in your life as a list of obstacles and challenges that have tested your ability to grow and prosper. Every obstacle and challenge can make you stronger and wiser and a winner, or you can give in to defeat, hopelessness, and death. God promises to give you the strength you need to endure any obstacle and promises that you will never be tested beyond your ability to endure. There is no need for fear where there is love and faith. So imagine yourself in your everyday life, waking up with certain challenges that all of us have sooner or later. We fight for what we want and what we believe in, no matter if it is in the past, present, or the future. If you have an issue with children, finances, a job, or even your health, accept that it is your responsibility to deal with it, with God's guaranteed help. You cannot continue to be trapped inside yourself, afraid to grow and improve your life. If you are a man, you serve a greater purpose because your children have their own obstacles in growing up. Part of your daily assignment is to guide them through their challenges. They are a part of your daily opportunity to teach them how to face their problems with courage, to grow from their experiences, and gradually to take on more and more responsibility for their own lives.

All of us are responsible for finding fulfillment in our own lives, to discover self, to grow from facing our challenges, knowing that God provides whatever is needed for us to succeed so long as we are not going against His will for our lives. As the purpose of each obstacle and opportunity is for personal growth, the purpose of one job is to train you for the next level until you work up to becoming the manager or the CEO of the company. A job is only a step that you must take to get to your final destination because the only way you will appreciate success is to know how you got there. In other words, what you learn in your journey strengthens you and prepares you for the next challenging opportunity for growth.

4. Knowing Your Gift

Every one of us in this world was born with a gift, talent, or some unique ability. It is up to each one of us to find it to create the best future. In order to find that future, we must first understand who we are, why we were created, and what makes us special. During these different stages that we pass through, we discover more about the ways we should live. I believe the path that leads to the greatest good lies in Christ. When we were born, we were given some of the greatest gifts: love, life, the ability to discover our purpose for existing, and the ability to grow and prosper. Every time we have used these gifts and special skills, we have prospered; and for every time we have applied effort, we have grown, flourished, expanded, enlarged, and become what God intends for all of us to become—successful in His image.

How can we look in the mirror everyday but never see the gifts God has given us from birth? We were born to prosper, to expand our scientific knowledge, to create new ideas or goods or services in order to improve our lives. We were born with the gift of greatness for your mother and father to discover, develop, nurture, and enjoy. These skills and talents are for you to use and share with the world to provide a better life for all. God gave you your gift, and without Him we cannot prosper. If not for God's grace, how else could we have known at the moment of birth that you could survive? How else could you have known at the moment of exiting the womb to take your first breath without being told? And a few months later, how else could you have known that your arms were strong enough to crawl without anyone else's example to imitate? How else could you have known that your legs were strong enough to stand and to walk? You even knew to walk without help; and when it was something you wanted, you knew when to laugh and cry to get it, without knowing why emotions are useful.

We were created by the greatest scientist, mathematician, and teacher in the history of this universe to grow, prosper, create life, and discover our individual gifts. All of us are images of God, created with a scientific mindset to invent, create, discover, enhance, and make difficult things simpler in order to progress. Some of you were given the opportunity to recognize your gifts at a very early age so you do not have any excuse or confusion about knowing your purpose. Most of us needed more time to discover our gifts and learn how to use them to make the best life.

I cannot tell you what do with your gift or tell you what your purpose is, but I do know that all of us were born a genius, gifted with senses, creative abilities, tools, and powers to perform, think, act, and love. A genius is someone who can turn a difficult situation into a simple one. When you think simply, you get simple answers. All these gifts were given to us to serve God by serving each other, helping each other to prosper. A genius is creative and discovers that creativity is of God; he thrives where there is love, encouragement, and enhancement. A genius improves on God's creation throughout history, starting from the first six days of existence in all areas of life—food, medicine, knowledge, vision, humanity, fashion, faith, and color. It is our assignment to be good stewards of all we have been given and to enhance and contribute to life for everyone's benefit.

Recognizing What You Have Been Taught

What we receive at birth enhances our life, encourages our decisions, and empowers our actions, thoughts, and visions. We come into this world fully equipped. Because many of us have not been taught that we were born with gifts, we have not used them. The greatest gift is the need to seek your God so He can show you your path. Success is within reach. Keep reaching. You have been told that America owes you. Not true. Show your receipt proving that you have already received it. You have been told that success comes only in white, but there are many flavors. Pick one that best suits you. Otherwise, do not get caught in the room with your gift without knowing that you have the power within you to unwrap it and use it.

There are so many things that you must understand about your gift and your purpose. God did not create you so you would not use your mind, and He surely did not create you for the purpose of begging and waiting on others for a handout. A good friend of mine, T. M. G., once said, "You have the independent ability to control your own destiny." So let us control it. What makes America so great is that each one of us has the creative ability to become whatever we want and to strive for the greatest and highest goals known to mankind. It has been the lack of good leadership and misunderstanding of what is CHANGE that has changed your course and altered your destiny. Our biggest problem has been the historical distractions of slavery, oppression, racism, and political parties. But none of these things has anything to do with you succeeding now. Their past is not your past, nor is it your future; but no effort can bring you to repeating a different kind of painful past if you do not get up and make something happen now. Your ancestors' past has hindered your future because you have refused to be independent. You have allowed your gifts to slip away because you refused to develop and use them. There are so many of us that have not found our gifts so we have failed to enhance our lives by following our dreams. There are so many of us that do not realize that a dream is not just a dream; a dream is a vision that you work hard at to turn into reality.

Looking over the Confusion

You see, there is a reason for everything, and every reason has a purpose, and every individual is given a purpose and gifts at birth. This bundle of gifts will make us miserable until we realize that God expects us to develop them and use them to make life happy and fulfilled for ourselves and others. Dr. King once said, "We must learn that to expect God to do everything while we do nothing is not faith but superstition." We have to recognize our gifts to realize our greatness.

Believe in your effort. Your gifts blossom in the confidence that comes from God who believes in you. We have to believe in ourselves enough to know that what we believe in gives us the power to expand our lives. All human beings have the inborn ability and strength to become the best at their gifts to create opportunities for themselves and others. All of us were given gifts at birth: love and the ability to encourage and inspire others who lack the strength and the knowledge. The requirement is simple: learn to think, and then learn to think outside the box to guide your own life. Too many of us have been conditioned to see ourselves in a negative light. We have allowed others to confuse us. When looking at ourselves in a mirror, we do not recognize what is really there, a beautiful child of God created in His own image. Whatsoever a person thinks of himself, later, he becomes. When we have not recognized who we are and what our gifts, talents, and purpose can become, we tend to settle for less because we are afraid.

Greatest Gift

Love is the greatest gift, more powerful than man or money. It is the gift of all gifts; without love, we are nothing. Putting too much love in others is the reason why many of us have not found our gifts, and sadly, many of us have not tried very hard to love self first so we have not expected much in return. Many of us have not been taught that a gift is good because it brings happiness to our lives and to the lives of others. So many are left confused because they have tried nothing and thus achieved nothing. It is through the love for Christ that all things are made possible. How can you have faith in God but not follow His laws? Love is not an emotion; it is making a choice to take action. As long as you are seriously trying, you will prosper. Faith without love is just faith with no effort. If we compare love with faith in any form, we will arrive at the same conclusion: love comes first, then growth and prosperity. In 1 Corinthians 13, it states that love is the greatest gift of all. God blesses us when we choose to love Him, ourselves, and others. There are many of us that are afraid to try because we do not love ourselves. We would rather live vicariously through others' successes and claim that as our purpose. We would rather see others grow than strive for our own greatness. Once you can apply love to all things—your confidence, your ambition, and your efforts—then you will be able to see your destiny fulfilled in front of your very own eyes.

Giving Thanks

Give thanks to the Gift Giver for the gifts you have been given, and focus on achieving your destiny because you have been touched by God. There are other Black American leaders, such as Herman Cain, Allen West, Condoleezza Rice, Clarence Thomas, that tried to warn you, but you called them sellouts and traitors, among other names. There have also been others who do not look like us, who cannot understand why we have not taken advantage of what America has to offer. The Republican Party, Rush Limbaugh, Glenn Beck, Sean Hannity, and a host of others have tried to warn you, but you called them racists. They cannot understand why we continue to listen to those who continually use racism to divide us and to divide you from your gift.

Today I encourage you to stop listening to what has hindered your growth and stop teaching your children to be afraid of other races and the laws that were intended to protect our gifts. Teach them how to live their life, love others, and more important, teach them how to live out their gift and their purpose.

Until next time,
Make 'em remember you.

ENDNOTES

Awakening: The True Beginning

1. Judy Hull Moore, *The History of Our United States, Third Edition* (1990), 206.

2. Zeke Miller, "Don't Compare Me to the Almighty, Compare Me to the Alternative," Business Insiders, September 25, 2011, http://articles.businessinsider.com/2011-09-25/politics/30201080_1_gop-debate-pool-report-president-barack-obama#ixzz1cywIMcMl.

3. "School Prayer Case History," *All about History*, http://www.allabouthistory.org/school-prayer.htm

4. Todd Starnes, "Texas Lawmaker Calls for Congressional Probe into Ban of Christian Prayers at Military Funerals," Fox News, July 26, 2011, http://www.foxnews.com/politics/2011/07/26/texas-lawmaker-calls-for-congressional-probe-into-ban-christian-prayers-at/.

5. Madeleine Morgenstern, "Obama at a Prayer Breakfast: Jesus Would Want Us to Tax the Rich," *The Blaze*, http://www.theblaze.com/stories/obama-at-prayer-breakfast-jesus-would-tax-the-rich/.

6. David Barton, "America's Most Biblically Hostile U. S. President," Wall Builders, February 29, 2012, http://www.wallbuilders.com/LIBissuesArticles.asp?id=106938.

Additional Notes

For more information on school fighting ACLU over prayer banner, go to:http://radio.foxnews.com/2011/03/08/school-vows-to-fight-aclu-over-prayer-banner/.

Deficiency: A Father's Failure

1. Paul A. Cimbala, *Under the Guardianship of the Nation: the Freedmen's Bureau and the Reconstruction of Georgia, 1865–1870* (1997).

2. Bruce E. Baker, *What Reconstruction Meant: Historical Memory in the American South* (2007), http://en.wikipedia.org/wiki/Reconstruction_era_of_the_United_States.

3. *Wikipedia*, http://en.wikipedia.org/wiki/Enforcement_Acts.

4. Richard Wormser, "Enforcement Act," http://www.pbs.org/wnet/jimcrow/stories_events_enforce.html.

5. *Wikipedia*, http://en.wikipedia.org/wiki/History_of_the_United_States_House_of_Representatives.

6. *Wikipedia*, http://en.wikipedia.org/wiki/Party_leaders_of_the_United_States_Senate.

7. Borgna Brunner and Elissa Haney, "Civil Right Timeline: Milestone in the modern civil rights movement," *Info Please*, http://www.infoplease.com/spot/civilrightstimeline1.html.

8. *Wikipedia*, http://en.wikipedia.org/wiki/Brown_v._Board_of_Education.

9. "People & Events: Citizens' Councils—Uptown Clan," *PBS – American Experience*, http://www.pbs.org/wgbh/amex/till/peopleevents/e_councils.html.

10. "The Little Rock Nine," *Civil Rights Movement Veterans*, http://www.crmvet.org/tim/timhis57.htm#1957lrsd.

11. *Wikipedia*, http://en.wikipedia.org/wiki/Watts_Riots.

12. *Wikipedia*, http://en.wikipedia.org/wiki/Bobby_Frank_Cherry.

13. Maryanne Vollers, *Ghosts of Mississippi: The Murder of Medgar Evers, the Trials of Byron de la Beckwith, and the Haunting of the New South* (Little, Brown, 1995), http://books.google.com/books?id=Zix1QgAACAAJ.

14. *Wikipedia*, http://en.wikipedia.org/wiki/Civil_Rights_Act_of_1957.

15. http://www.usccr.gov/.

16. *New World Encyclopedia*, "Jim Crow Laws," http://www.newworldencyclopedia.org/entry/Jim_Crow_laws.

17. Bonnie Bullard London, *Georgia and the American Experience* (1976), 352.

18. Library of Congress, "Primary Document in American History: Missouri Compromise," http://www.loc.gov/rr/program/bib/ourdocs/Missouri.html.

19. Robert W. Johansson, *Stephen A. Douglas* (Oxford UP, 1973), 374-400, http://www.ourdocuments.gov/doc.php?flash=true&doc=28.

20. J. G. Randall and David Donald, *A House Divided: The Civil War and Reconstruction,* 2nd ed. (Boston: D.C. Heath and Company, 1961), 107–114.

21. United State Senate, http://www.senate.gov/artandhistory/history/minute/Civil_Rights_Filibuster_Ended.htm.

22. "A Solid Leader for Solid South," *LIFE*, May 21, 1956, 34, http://books.google.com/books?id=q0gEAAAAMBAJ&pg=PA34.

23. Ball, *Hugo L. Black*, 16, 50.

24. Margaret Truman, *Harry S. Truman* (William Morrow and Co., 1973), 429,http://howard53545.wordpress.com/2007/07/25/was-harry-s-truman-a-member-of-the-kkk/.

25. "Segregation at All Costs: Bull Connor and the Civil Rights Movement," YouTube, April 8, 2011, http://www.youtube.com/watch?v=j9kT1yO4MGg>.

26. http://www.historylearningsite.co.uk/john_kennedy_and_civil_rights.htm.

27. http://www.senate.gov/artandhistory/history/common/briefing/Filibuster_Cloture.htm.

28. http://en.wikipedia.org/wiki/J._William_Fulbright.

29. "Southern Manifesto," http://www.pbs.org/wnet/supremecourt/rights/sources_document2.html.

30. http://www.senate.gov/artandhistory/history/common/briefing/Filibuster_Cloture.htm.

31. *Wikipedia,* http://en.wikipedia.org/wiki/J._William_Fulbright.

32. "Southern Manifesto," http://www.pbs.org/wnet/supremecourt/rights/sources_document2.html.

33. *Wikipedia,* http://en.wikipedia.org/wiki/James_Earl_Ray.

34. Hampton Sides, *Hellhound on His Trail: The Stalking of Martin Luther King Jr. and the Hunt for His Assassin* (New York: Doubleday, 2010), 60.

35. *Wikipedia,* http://en.wikipedia.org/wiki/George_Wallace#cite_note-Woods_On_Fire_quotes-16.

36. Daniel Mccabe (writer, director, producer), Paul Stekler (writer, director, producer), Steve Fayer (writer), *George Wallace: Settin' the Woods on Fire,* (Boston: American Experience, 2000), http://www.imdb.com/title/tt0240534/.

37. Maggie Riechers, "Racism to Redemption: The Path of George Wallace," *Humanities,* March/April 2000, http://www.neh.gov/news/humanities/2000-03/wallace.html.

38. "George Wallace: Settin' the Woods on Fire: Wallace Quotes," Public Broadcasting Service, *The American Experience,* (WGBH), 2000, http://www.pbs.org/wgbh/amex/wallace/sfeature/quotes.html.

39. Michael J. Klarman, "*Brown v. Board*: 50 Years Later," *Humanities: the Magazine of the National Endowment for the Humanities*, March/April 2004, http://www.neh.gov/news/humanities/2004-03/brown.html.

40. "MLK Was a Republican, Affirmed by Niece Dr. Alveda C. King," National Black Republican Associations, http://www.nationalblackrepublicans.com/Videos.

Additional Notes

For more information on the Confederate States, see Wikipedia: http://en.wikipedia.org/wiki/Confederate_States_of_America.

For more information on President Obama's connection with Bill Ayers, view the video from CNN at: http://www.youtube.com/watch?v=XDU_KFw-q6E.

For more information on the Kansas-Nebraska act, read Nicole Etcheson's book, *Bleeding Kansas: Contested Liberty in the Civil War Era* (2006), Chapter 1.

The Trap: Isolated from the Truth

1. Craig Schneider and Tammy Joyner, "Housing Crisis Reaches Full Boil in East Point; 62 Injured," *Atlanta Journal-Constitution*, August 11, 2010, http://www.ajc.com/news/atlanta/housing-crisis-reaches-full-589653.html?printArticle=y.

2. *Wikipedia*, http://en.wikipedia.org/wiki/Southern_Association_of_Colleges_and_Schools.

3. *Wikipedia*, http://en.wikipedia.org/wiki/Confederate_States_of_America.

4. *Wikipedia*, http://en.wikipedia.org/wiki/107th_United_States_Congress.

5. Heather Vogell, "Investigation into APS Cheating Finds Unethical Behavior across Every Level," *Atlanta Journal-Constitution*, http://www.ajc.com/news/atlanta/atlanta-public-schools-cheating-1026035.html.

6. John Stossel, "Stupid in America," http://www.youtube.com/watch?v=OGNz0Y9vrBo&feature=related.

7. Salma, "Steve Jobs in 1996: 'What's Wrong with Education Can't Be Fixed with Technology,'" *Tech Journal*, January 19, 2012, http://thetech-journal.com/tech-news/steve-jobs-in-1996-whats-wrong-with-education-cant-be-fixed-with-technology.xhtml.

8. http://www.politifact.com/truth-o-meter/statements/2011/mar/15/republican-national-committee-republican/rnc-said-unions-raised-400-million-obama-2008/.

9. Sam Hananel, "Union Gearing Up to Spend Big in 2012 Election," Associated Press, February 22, 2012, http://finance.yahoo.com/news/unions-gearing-spend-big-2012-080108771.html.

10. Rush Limbaugh, "Educator: Parents Don't Know Best," February 15, 2012, http://www.rushlimbaugh.com/daily/2012/02/15/educator_parents_don_t_know_best.

11. *Wikipedia*, http://en.wikipedia.org/wiki/96th_United_States_Congress#Major_legislation.

12. Palm Beach Post, October 18, 1979 http://news.google.com/newspapers?id=0sZUAAAAIBAJ&sjid=ejsNAAAAIBAJ&pg=1984,3959160&hl=en.

13. "Chronology of the School Prayer Debate," http://www.churchandstate.us/church-state/chronology.htm.

14. http://rankingamerica.wordpress.com/tag/education/.

15. http://rankingamerica.wordpress.com/2009/03/24/the-us-ranks-34th-in-math-progress/.

16. James Levulis, "Obama Signs Healthy Hungry Free Kids Act," NCC News Online, December 16, 2010, https://nccnews.expressions.syr.edu/?p=2972.

17. "Federal Stimulus Dollars Pay for the School Lunch Food Police," Fox Nation, February 15, 2012, http://pjmedia.com/tatler/2012/02/15/federal-stimulus-dollars-pay-for-the-school-lunch-food-police/?utm_source=twitterfeed&utm_medium=twitter.

18. "Van Jones to Young People, 'You Are Gods, Forget Respecting Older People," Breit Bart TV, http://www.breitbart.tv/van-jones-to-young-people-you-are-gods-forget-respecting-older-people/.

19. Katherine Kehoe, "Obama: Tuition Costs a Priority," *Badger Herald*, October 6, 2008, http://badgerherald.com/news/2008/10/06/obama_tuition_costs_.php.

20. Buzz Patterson, "Obama Connection," Human Events, September 9, 2010, http://www.humanevents.com/article.php?id=38917.

21. Glenn Beck, "The Man Who Broke the Bank of England," http://www.youtube.com/watch?v=IXKoYO9chDA.

22. "Glenn Beck: Making of the Puppet Master," Fox News, November 12, 2010, http://www.foxnews.com/story/0,2933,602163,00.html.

23. "Glenn Beck: Five Step Plan," Fox News, November 11, 2010, http://www.foxnews.com/story/0,2933,602143,00.html.

24. Alex Chadwick, "Remembering Tuskegee," *The Recording Report*, NPR, November 27, 2011, http://www.npr.org/programs/morning/features/2002/jul/tuskegee/ http://www.infoplease.com/spot/bhmtuskegee1.html.

25. *Miss Evers Boys* (HBO, 2001).

26. Examining Tuskegee, http://examiningtuskegee.com/timeline.html.

27. Alex Chadwick, "Remembering Tuskegee," *The Recording Report*, NPR, November 27, 2011, http://www.npr.org/programs/morning/features/2002/jul/tuskegee/ http://www.infoplease.com/spot/bhmtuskegee1.html.

28. *Miss Evers Boys* (HBO, 2001).

Additional Notes

For more information on the government's ideas and plans about nutrition, visit: http://www.whitehouse.gov/sites/default/files/Child_Nutrition_Fact_Sheet_12_10_10.pdf.

The Indoctrination: The Making of a Patient

1. Allen C. Guelzo, *Lincoln and Douglas: The Debates That Defined America* (2008), 273–277.

2. J. G. Randall and David Donald, *A House Divided: The Civil War and Reconstruction,* 2nd ed. (Boston: D.C. Heath and Company, 1961), 107–114.

3. http://www.csrees.usda.gov/about/offices/legis/secondmorrill.html.

4. http://www.portchesterryenaacp.org/about/history/timeline/index.htm.

5. *Wikipedia,* http://en.wikipedia.org/wiki/Everett_Dirksen.

6. Free Republic/April 20, 2008/ http://www.freerepublic.com/focus/f-chat/2004277/posts.

7. Benjamin R. Freed, February 22, 2012, http://dcist.com/2012/02/obama_laura_bush_gray_break_ground.php.

Additional Notes

For more information on the Lincoln-Douglas debates, go to: http://en.wikipedia.org/wiki/Lincoln-Douglas_debates_of_1858#cite_note-6 (also notes 7, 8 and 9).

Their Curse: The Failed Legacy

1. "Jesse Jackson Jr. Says Way Out of the Unemployment Crisis Is to Change the Constitution So Every Ghetto Kid Gets an iPod and a Laptop," *Naked Emperor News*, March 7, 2011, http://www.theblaze.com/stories/jesse-jackson-jr-says-way-out-of-the-unemployment-crisis-is-to-change-the-constitutional-so-every-ghetto-kid-gets-an-ipod-and-a-laptop/.

2. Naimah Jabali-Nash, "Bishop Eddie Long Scandal: Ga. Church Admits Trips, Nothing Else," CBS News, http://www.cbsnews.com/8301-504083_162-20022204-504083.html.

3. Thomas Cloud, "Pelosi Vows to Stand With Obama Against Catholic Church; Says Decision Forcing Catholics to Act Against Faith Was Very Courageous," CNS News, February 2, 2012, http:// cnsnews.com/news/article/pelosi-vows-stand-obama-against-catholic-church-says-decision-forcing-catholics-act.

4. Joel Gehrke, "Holder To Brief Pastors On Campaign 2012," Washington Examiner, May 29, 2012, http://campaign2012.washington-examiner.com/blogs/beltway-confidential/holder-brief-black-pastors-campaign-2012/567501.

5. Herbert Pinnock, "Eddie Long Demands $1M Repayment from Accusers," *Christian Post*, October 1, 2011, *http://www.christianpost.com/news/eddie-long-demands-1m-repayment-from-accusers-57001/.*

6. "Special Report on the Banking Crisis, Part 1," Fox News, September 9, 2003, http://www.youtube.com/watch?v=VgctSIL8Lhs&feature=player_embedded.

7. "Special Report on the Banking Crisis, Part 2," Fox News, September 24, 2008, http://www.youtube.com/watch?v=VgctSIL8Lhs&feature=player_embedded.

8. *Wikipedia*, http://en.wikipedia.org/wiki/110th_United_States_Congress.

9. Nice Deb, "The White House Warned Congress about Fannie Mae Freddie Mac 17 Times in 2008, Alone," September, 21, 2008, http://nicedeb.wordpress.com/2008/09/21/the-white-house-warned-congress-about-fannie-mae-freddie-mac-17-times-in-2008-alone/.

10. "Biden: It's Time to Blame Obama, Not Bush, for Economy," Newsmax Wires, September 29, 2011, http://www.newsmax.com/InsideCover/Biden-blame-Obama Bush/2011/09/29/id/412762?s=al&promo_code=D286-1.

11. Ted Manna, "Obama Signs $787-Billion Stimulus Package in Struggling Denver," *American Reporter*, September 26, 2011, http://www.american-reporter.com/4,305/658.html.

12. "Solyndra Not Sole Firm to Hit Rock Bottom Despite Stimulus Funding," Fox News, September 15, 2011, http://www.foxnews.com/politics/2011/09/15/despite-stimulus-funding-solyndra-and-4-other-companies-have-hit-rock-bottom/.

Additional Notes

For more on the bank crisis, see the article, "Democrats blocked reformed of Freddie and Fannie" http://wthrockmorton.com/2008/09/25/democrats-blocked-reformed-of-freddie-and-fannie-received-most-money-from-freddie-and-fannie/.

The Leaders: Gradually Selling Out

1. Laura Fitzpatrick, "China's One-Child Policy," Time World, http://www.time.com/time/world/article/0,8599,1912861,00.html.

2. *Wikipedia*, http://en.wikipedia.org/wiki/One-child_policy.

3. Kenneth Timmerman, *Shakedown: Exposing the Real Jesse Jackson*, (2003).

4. "Jesse Jackson and MLK's 'Precious Blood,'" WVW News, April 4, 2008, http://www.wnd.com/?pageId=13339#ixzz1hEYihWX4.

5. Charles Johnson, "Jesse Jackson Sr.'s Role in the Housing Crisis," December 30, 2009, http://www.claremontconservative.com/2009/12/jesse-jackson-srs-role-in-housing.html.

6. *Pagones v. Maddox* et al.

7. James S. Kunen, "Trials of Tawana: The Scandal behind the Tawana Brawley Rape Case," July 4, 1988, http://www.people.com/people/archive/article/0,,20099354,00.html.

8. Alan Feuer, "Sharpton's Debt in Brawley Defamation Is Paid by Supporters," June 15, 2001, http://www.nytimes.com/2001/06/15/nyregion/sharpton-s-debt-in-brawley-defamation-is-paid-by-supporters.html.

9. "Winner in Brawley Suit Says Victory is Bittersweet," CNN, http://web.archive.org/web/20070320025016/http://www.cnn.com/US/9807/13/brawley.verdict.02/.

10. Wayne Barnett, "Sharpton's Affirmative-Action Win," Daily Beast, July 27, 2011, http://www.thedailybeast.com/articles/2011/07/27/al-sharpton-affirmative-action-beneficiary-of-the-nbc-comcast-merger.html.

11. Madeleine Morgenstern, "Do You Want Al Sharpton to Have His Own MSNBC? Black Journalists Don't," *The Blaze*, August 7, 2011, http://www.theblaze.com/stories/do-you-want-al-sharpton-to-have-his-own-msnbc-show-black-journalists-dont/.

12. "Thousands Rally to Support Jena," Associated Press, WSBTV, September 20, 2007, http://www.wsbtv.com/news/14155988/detail.html.

13. Andrew Stiles, *Washington Free Beacon*, March 27, 2012, http://freebeacon.com/registered-dem-killed-trayvon/.

14. Joegerarden, "Pelosi: Food Stamps & Unemployment Give Us the 'Biggest Bang for the Buck,'" http://www.youtube.com/watch?v=4t-eycEKXNs.

15. "We Need to Pass Health Care Bill to Find Out What's in It, Breit Bart TV, http://www.breitbart.tv/nancy-pelosi-we-need-to-pass-health-care-bill-to-find-out-whats-in-it/.

16. "16,500 More IRS Agents Needed to Enforce Obamacare," *Examiner*, http://washingtonexaminer.com/politics/beltway-confidential/2010/03/16500-more-irs-agents-needed-enforce-obamacare/5655.

17. *Wikipedia,* http://en.wikipedia.org/wiki/National_Defense_Authorization_Act_for_Fiscal_Year_2012.

18. US Government Accountability Office "Cost Impact Health Care Reform and the Extension of Department Coverage," DOD Healthcare September 26,2011, http://www.gao.gov/products/GAO-11-837R.

19. Sheryl Gay Stolberg, "Obama Signs Don't Ask Don't Tell," *New York Times,* December 22, 2010, http://www.nytimes.com/2010/12/23/us/politics/23military.html.

20. Margaret Talev, "Obama Signs Federal Gay Rights Laws," *McClatchy Newspapers,* October 29, 2009, http://www.collegiatetimes.com/stories/14562/obama-signs-federal-gay-rights-law.

21. "Updated: Obama's New Executive Order = 'Dream Act,'" *The Blaze,* August 20 2011, http://www.theblaze.com/stories/obama-orders-his-own-version-of-the-dream-act-video/.

22. "Amish, Muslims Exempt from Obamacare Mandate?," Fox Nation, March 24, 2010, http://nation.foxnews.com/culture/2010/03/24/amish-muslims-exempt-obamacare-mandate#ixzz1exvs6MC5.

23. Mac Slavo, "Obama Phone: Gov to Spend $2.4 Billion on Millions of Free Phones in 2012," SHTF Plan, February 9, 2012, http://www.shtfplan.com/headline-news/free-obamaphone-gov-to-spend-2-4-billion-on-millions-of-free-phones-in-2012_02092012.

24. Richard Wormser, *The Rise and Fall of Jim Crow* (2003), 82.

25. Boyce Watkins, "President Obama Meets with Sharpton, Morial Jealous on Black Unemployment, February 10, 2010, http://www.bvonmoney.com/2010/02/10/al-sharpton-marc-morial-ben-jealous-obama/.

26. "Al Sharpton in Albuquerque, New Mexico," YouTube, http://www.youtube.com/watch?v=JMuNEb6Nns4.

27. Boyce Watkins, "President Obama Meets with Sharpton, Morial Jealous on Black Unemployment, February 10, 2010, http://www.bvonmoney.com/2010/02/10/al-sharpton-marc-morial-ben-jealous-obama/.

28. Deniise Steward, "Smiley, Sharpton Spar over Black Agenda, Obama," BlackAmericaWeb.com, February 24, 2010, http://www.blackamericaweb.com/?q=articles/news/moving_america_news/16617.

29. *Wikipedia*, http://en.wikipedia.org/wiki/Civil_War_(United_States)#Slavery.

Additional Notes

For more information on the killing of Gadhafi's children, see the article, "Obama Ordered Bombing In Libya Kills Gadhafi's Son, Underage Grandchildren and Destroyed School For Disabled Children, " May 21, 2011 at: http://www.judiciaryreport.com/obama_ordered_bombing_in_libya_kills_gadhafi_son_grandkids_and_disabled_school.htm.

For more information on Obama and Tony Rezko, go to: http://stmarie.wordpress.com/2008/10/06/barack-obama-and-tony-rezko-a-convicted-felon/.

For more information on Van Jones, see Jonathon M. Seidl's article, "Van Jones Group Uses Kids Video to Push Universal Health Care, Higher Taxes," August 10, 2011, at: http://www.theblaze.com/stories/van-jones-group-uses-kids-video-to-push-universal-health-care-higher-taxes/.

For more information on Mubarak being asked to step down, see Anthony Shadid's article, "Obama Suggests Mubarak Should Step Down Now," *New York Times*, February 2, 2011, at: http://www.ndtv.com/article/world/obama-suggests-mubarak-should-step-down-now-82967&cp.

Intent: Connecting the Dots

1. "The man who broke the Bank of England," BBC News, December 6, 1998, http://news.bbc.co.uk/2/hi/business/229012.stm.

2. Arlen Williams, "On Being God, from the Mouth of George Soros," October 6, 2010, http://gulagbound.com/6356/on-being-god-from-the-mouth-of-george-soros/.

3. "Is George Soros Funding Wall Street Protests?," Independent Word, October13,2011,http://independentword.com/2011/10/is-george-soros-funding-wall-street-protests/.

4. Tiffany Gabbay for the *Blaze*, "Meet Soros-Funded Domestic Terrorist Brett Kimberlin Whose 'Job' Is Terrorizing Bloggers into Silence," May 25, 2012, http://www.theblaze.com/stories/readymeet-soros-funded-domestic-terrorist-brett-kimberlin-whose-job-is-terrorizing-bloggers-into-silence/.

5. Rachel Ehrenfeld and Shawn Macomber, "George Soros: The 'God' Who Carries around Some Dangerous Demons," October 4, 2004, http://gulagbound.com/6356/on-being-god-from-the-mouth-of-george-soros/.

6. Devonia Smith, "Glenn Beck: George Soros Is 'Playing God' with US for New World Order," *Examiner*, November 11, 2010, http://www.examiner.com/political-transcripts-in-national/glenn-beck-george-soros-is-playing-god-with-us-for-new-world-order-video.

7. "The Puppet Master Soros," Glenn Beck Part 2, YouTube, November 9, 2010, /http://www.youtube.com/watch?v=tn_KAiYx4X8&feature=related.

8. Glenn Beck, "Who Is the Twelfth Imam?," *The Blaze*, February 17, 2011, http://www.theblaze.com/stories/beck-who-is-the-12th-imam/.

9. "12th Imam—Anointed Ruler?," *Popular Issues*, January 3, 2012, http://www.allaboutpopularissues.org/12th-imam.htm.

10. *Wikipedia*, http://en.wikipedia.org/wiki/Muhammad_al-Mahdi.

11. "12th Imam—Anointed Ruler?," *Popular Issues*, January 3, 2012, http://www.allaboutpopularissues.org/12th-imam.htm.

12. "Marx and Engels 1848 Communist Manifesto," Chapter Two, http://www.marxists.org/archive/marx/works/1848/communist-manifesto/ch02.htm.

13. *After Alinsky: Community Organizing in Illinois* (Springfield, Illinois: Sangamon State University, 1989), 123–152.

14. *Wikipedia*, Bill Ayers, "Statement made in 2001," http://en.wikipedia.org/wiki/Bill_Ayers.

15. "Obama Helped Fund Alinsky Academy," *World Daily Exclusive*, March 18, 2010, http://www.crossroad.to/Quotes/communism/alinsky.htm.

16. http://factcheck.org/2008/10/acorn-accusations/.

17. Frank Pastore, *Townhall*, October 9, 2008, http://townhall.com/columnists/frankpastore/2008/10/09/obama,_ayers,_and_the_politics_of_intimidation/page/full/.

18. "ACORN will shape my agenda," *The Obama File*, http://www.theobamafile.com/ObamaACORN.htm.

19. Bud White, "Sleeper Cell: ACORN, Obama, and the Housing Crisis," *No Quarter*, October 10, 2008, http://www.noquarterusa.net/blog/5348/sleeper-cell-acorn-obama-and-the-housing-crisis/.

20. "ACORN will shape my agenda," *The Obama File*, http://www.theobamafile.com/ObamaACORN.htm.

21. Bud White, "Sleeper Cell: ACORN, Obama, and the Housing Crisis," *No Quarter*, October 10, 2008, http://www.noquarterusa.net/blog/5348/sleeper-cell-acorn-obama-and-the-housing-crisis/.

22. Frank Pastore, *Townhall*, October 9, 2008, http://townhall.com/columnists/frankpastore/2008/10/09/obama,_ayers,_and_the_politics_of_intimidation/page/full/.

23. "ACORN will shape my agenda," *The Obama File*, http://www.theobamafile.com/ObamaACORN.htm.

24. Bud White, "Sleeper Cell: ACORN, Obama, and the Housing Crisis," *No Quarter*, October 10, 2008, http://www.noquarterusa.net/blog/5348/sleeper-cell-acorn-obama-and-the-housing-crisis/.

25. "ACORN will shape my agenda," *The Obama File*, http://www.theobamafile.com/ObamaACORN.htm.

26. Pam for Right Voices, September 17, 2008, http://rightvoices.com/2008/09/17/acorn-fannie-mae-freddie-mac-barack-obamas-finance-chair-penny-pritzker-all-tied-to-the-sub-prime-meltdown/.

27. http://patft.uspto.gov/netacgi/nph-Parser?Sect1=PTO1&Sect2=HITOFF&d=PALL&p=1&u=%2Fnetahtml%2FPTO%2Fsrchnum.htm&r=1&f=G&l=50&s1=6904336.PN.&OS=PN/6904336&RS=PN/6904336.

28. Whitney Ray, "Turtle Tunnel," WJHG NBCNews, June 17, 2009, http://www.wjhg.com/news/headlines/48278457.html.

29. Tom Coburn, "$7.5 million in stimulus funds may go to fix useless trout ladder," February 24, 2010, http://coburn.senate.gov/public/index.cfm?p=News&ContentRecord_id=01fdde0a-802a-23ad-4f79-61c7304594cb.

30. Damien Baldino, "Your stimulus money at work: $3 million for fish ladders," *Providence Conservative Examiner*, http://www.examiner.com/conservative-in-providence/your-stimulus-money-at-work-3-million-for-fish-ladders.

31. *Wikipedia*, http://en.wikipedia.org/wiki/Cloward%E2%80%93Piven_strategy.

32. Terence P. Jeffrey, "Financial Disclosure: Obama Not Bullish on Long-Term U.S. Debt," CNS News, May 17, 2011, http://cnsnews.com/news/article/financial-disclosure-obama-not-bullish-long-term-us-debt.

33. Vicki Needham, "Senators back ambitious trade agenda with Europe," *The Hill*, February 23, 2012, http://thehill.com/blogs/on-the-money/801-economy/166599-pelosis-net-worth-rises-62-percent-.

34. "Barack Obama and Tony Rezko, a Convicted Felon," *St. Marie*, October 6, 2008, http://stmarie.wordpress.com/2008/10/06/barack-obama-and-tony-rezko-a-convicted-felon/.

35. Chuck Justice, "Valarie Jarrett Runs the White House," *Habledash*, December 22, 2010, /http://habledash.com/the-nook/3456/white-house-insider-valerie-jarrett-runs-the-white-house.

36. *Wikipedia,* http://en.wikipedia.org/wiki/Barbara_T._Bowman.

37. *Wikipedia,* http://en.wikipedia.org/wiki/Thomas_G._Ayers#cite_note-1.

38. Thomas G. Ayers and Barack Obama, http://watch.pair.com/synarchy-3.html.

39. http://keywiki.org/index.php/Vernon_Jarrett.

40. "Sam Webb on May Day and Class Struggle Today," Communist Party USA, May 2, 2012, http://www.cpusa.org/sam-webb-on-may-day-and-class-struggle-today/.

41. Barack Obama, *Dreams from My Father,* Chapters 4–5.

42. Jerome Corsi, "Postman: Ayers Family Put 'Foreigner' Obama through School," WND, March 19, 2012, /http://www.wnd.com/2012/03/postman-ayers-family-put-foreigner-obama-through-school/.

43. Shaun Waterman, "Drone Over U.S. get OK by Congress," *Washington Times,* February 7, 2012, http://www.washingtontimes.com/news/2012/feb/7/coming-to-a-sky-near-you/.

44. Raven Clabough, "Obama Signs United Nations Agenda 21," June 22, 2011, http://www.ronpaulforums.com/showthread.php?299917-Obama-Signs-United-Nations-Agenda-21-Related-Executive-Order.

45."Obama Speaks to the Muslim," YouTube, http://search.yahoo.com/search?ei=utf-8&fr=slv8-tyc8&p=video%20of%20obama%20in%20cairo&type=.

46. "Globe Poverty Act of 2007," *Crossroad,* http://www.crossroad.to/Quotes/law/global/poverty-act.htm.

47. *Wikipedia,* http://en.wikipedia.org/wiki/Global_Poverty_Act.

48. "Crisis & Protest in Egypt; President Obama, U.S. and the World React," *WordPress,* February 4, 2011, http://historymusings.wordpress.com/2011/02/04/february-4-2011-crisis-protest-in-egypt/.

49. "Quite Normal," *WordPress*, May 9, 2011, http://quitenormal.wordpress.com/2011/05/09/obama-to-forgive-1-billion-of-egyptian-debt/.

50. Richard W. Stevenson, "Official to Block Qaddafi to Farrakhan, *New York Times*, August 28, 1996, http://www.nytimes.com/1996/08/28/us/officials-to-block-qaddafi-gift-to-farrakhan.html.

51. *Daily Voice*, February 27, 2008, http://thedailyvoice.com/voice/2008/02/obama-renounces-farrakhan-000244.php.

52. Associated Press, April 29, 2008, http://www.msnbc.msn.com/id/24371827/ns/politics-decision_08/t/obama-strongly-denounces-former-pastor/.

53. "Mass Murder of Blacks in Libya," New World Order Live, September 6, 2011, http://www.youtube.com/watch?v=BHIZFmTwZv0.

54. "Attack on Gaddafi May Be Cut Short," My Gripe an Thing, http://www.mygripeanthing.com/2011/05/26/attack-on-gaddafi-may-be-cut-short/.

55. Scott Baker, "Who the Hell Do You Think You Are," *The Blaze*, March 19, 2011, http://www.theblaze.com/stories/farrakhan-warns-obama-on-libya-who-the-hell-do-you-think-your-are/.

56. Scott Baker, *The Blaze*, May 1, 2011, http://www.theblaze.com/stories/reports-gadhafi-survives-nato-airstrike-son-grandchildren-killed/.

57. Volubrjotr, Politcal Vel Craft, http://politicalvelcraft.org/2011/08/25/obama-is-done-we-must-undo-the-obama-mess-glass-steagall-will-nullify-the-bankers-fabricated-debt-called-socialism/.

58. Matthew Boyle, "Report – Documents: Obama Alleged Bribe Pal Had History with Jeremiah Wright," Fox Nation, May 16, 2012, http://nation.foxnews.com/rev-jeremiah-wright/2012/05/16/report-documents-obama-alleged-bribe-pal-had-history-jeremiah-wright#cb=fcbb0b545ccbfa&origin=http%3A%2F%2Fnation.foxnews.com%2Ff1be53df3694c54&relation=parent.parent&transport=postmessage&type=resize&height=21&ackData[id]=3.

59. John R. Parrkinson, "Lawmakers Sue President Obama over Illegal Libya War," ABC News, June 15, 2011, http://abcnews.go.com/blogs/politics/2011/06/lawmakers-sue-president-obama-over-illegal-libya-war/.

60. Robert Dreyfuss, *The Nation*, August 23, 2011, http://www.thenation.com/blog/162908/obamas-nato-war-oil-libya.

61. "Mass Murder of Blacks in Libya," New World Order Live, September 6, 2011, http://www.youtube.com/watch?v=BHIZFmTwZv0.

62. Brian, "Obama Administration Grants White House Meeting to 'Muslim Brotherhood' That Wants to Impose Sharia Law on Egypt," April 6, 2012, http://freedomslighthouse.net/2012/04/06/obama-administration-grants-white-house-meeting-to-muslim-brotherhood-that-wants-to-impose-sharia-law-on-egypt-video-report-4512/.

63. Joshua Hersh, "Obama: Syrian President Assad Must Step Down," *Huffington Post*, August 18, 2011, http://www.huffingtonpost.com/2011/08/18/obama-assad_n_930229.html (video).

64. Mackenzie Weinger, "Chavez: Obama a Clown President," *Fox News*, December 20, 2011, http://nation.foxnews.com/hugo-chavez/2011/12/21/chavez-obama-clown-president.

65. Thomas Erdbrink, "Iran to Return Downed US Drone to Obama, a Miniature Pink Plastic Replica," *Washington Post*, January 17, 2012, http://www.jihadwatch.org/2012/01/iran-to-return-downed-us-drone-to-obama-a-miniature-pink-plastic-replica.html.

66. "During Missile Defense Talk, Obama tells Medvedev He'll Have 'More Flexibility' after Election," *Fox News*, March 26, 2012, http://www.foxnews.com/politics/2012/03/26/obama-tells-medvedev-hell-have-more-flexibility-after-election-during-missile/.

67. http://www.youtube.com/watch?v=K6zpHtbM3hc.

68. "Russia Hires Exxon Mobil to Get Oil Obama Doesn't Want," Fox Nation, April 24, 2012, http://nation.foxnews.com/exxon-mobil/2012/04/24/russia-hires-exxon-mobil-get-oil-obama-doesnt-want.

69. Kenneth Rapoza, "How the Wall Street Journal Set off a Firestorm against Petrobras," *Forbes*, March 21, 2011, http://www.forbes.com/sites/kenrapoza/2011/03/21/how-the-wall-street-journal-set-off-a-firestorm-against-petrobras/.

70. "Obama Admin. Not Looking to Lower Gas Prices," Pirate Cove, February 29, 2012, http://www.thepiratescove.us/2012/02/29/obama-admin-not-looking-to-lower-gas-prices/.

71. Ed Morrissey, "Obama: 'I'd like higher gas prices, just not so quickly,'" Hot Air, http://hotair.com/archives/2008/06/11/obama-id-like-higher-gas-prices-just-not-so-quickly/.

72. http://www.youtube.com/watch?v=RrcGRljKHnI.

73. Oliver Knox, "Oil Is 'the Fuel of the Past,' Says President Obama," The Ticket, March 7, 2012, http://news.yahoo.com/blogs/ticket/oil-fuel-past-says-president-obama-212950677.html.

74. *Wikipedia*, http://en.wikipedia.org/wiki/Gas_prices.

Additional Notes

For more information on Bill Ayers and the Weather Underground, go to: http://www.time.com/time/magazine/article/0,9171,1848763,00.html.

For more information on Obama's connection with Bill Ayers, go to: http://en.wikipedia.org/wiki/Chicago_Annenberg_Challenge.

For more information on the Woods Fund of Chicago (2008), see the article, "About the Woods Fund: History of the Fund" at http://www.woodsfund.org/about/history.

For more information on Cloward-Piven go to: http://www.youtube.com/watch?v=qCIMbU4q1to.

For more information on President Obama's meeting with Muslims in the White House, see the article by Byron Tau for Politico, "Muslim Brotherhood Delegation Meets with White House Official," April 4, 2012, http://www.politico.com/politico44/2012/04/muslim-brotherhood-delegation-meets-with-white-house-119647.html.

For more information on fundraiser Tony Rezko, see the article by Mackenzie Weinger for Polictico, "Tony Rezko, Ex-fundraiser for Obama and Rob Blagojevich," November 22, 2011, http://www.polico.com/news/stories/1111/68935.html.

For more information on the bribe of Jeremiah Wright, see the article by Matthew Boyle, "Report Documents Obama Alleged Bribe Pal Had History with Jeremiah Wright," The Daily Caller, May 16, 2012, http://nation.foxnews.com/rev-jeremiah-wright/2012/05/16/report-documents-obama-alleged-bribe-pal-had-history-jeremiah-wright#ixzz1v501aHWe.

For more information on Rahm Emanuel begging Obama to alter his stance on health care , see the article by Brian Montopoli for CBSNews, "Rahm Emanuel 'Begged' Obama Not to Push Health Care." May 14, 2010, http://www.cbsnews.com/8301-503544_162-20005041-503544.html.

Their Media: They Control the Game

1. "President Obama Signs Executive Order Establishing Council of Governors," White House, http://www.whitehouse.gov/the-press-office/president-obama-signs-executive-order-establishing-council-governors.

2. Alex Newman, "Big Soros Money Linked to Occupy Wall Street," *New American*, October 5, 2011, http://www.thenewamerican.com/usnews/politics/9269-big-soros-money-linked-to-occupy-wall-street.

3. C. Vernon Coleman II, "Russell Simmons' Rush Card Investigated Over Hidden Fees," June 20, 2011, http://hiphopwired.com/2011/06/20/russel-simmons%e2%80%99-rush-card-investigated-over-hidden-fees/.

4. "Kanye Occupies Wall Street," http://www.youtube.com/watch?v=9y768coPoGo.

5. Jessica Derschowitz, "Russell Simmons Offered to Pay for Occupy Wall Street Cleanup," October 14, 2011, http://www.cbsnews.com/8301-31749_162-20120723-10391698.html.

6. Scott Baker, "Can You Answer Beck's Key Questions about 'Occupy Wall Street'?," *The Blaze*, October 18, 2011, http://www.theblaze.com/stories/can-you-answer-becks-key-questions-about-occupy-wall-street/.

7. Tina Trent, "Soros's Fingerprint on 'Occupy Wall Street,'" *The Soros Files*, January 25, 2012, http://sorosfiles.com/soros/2012/01/soros-fingerprints-on-occupy-wall-street.html.

8. "Limbaugh: Obama Setting Up Riots," Fox Nation, October 6, 2011, http://nation.foxnews.com/president-obama/2011/10/06/limbaugh-obama-setting-riots.

9. Christina Boyle, Emily Sher, Anjali Mullany, and Helen Kennedy, "Occupy Wall Street Protests: Police Make Arrests, Use Pepper Spray as Some Activists Storm Barricade," *NY Daily News*, May 10, 2011, http://www.nydailynews.com/ny_local/2011/10/05/2011-10-05_occupy_wall_street_protests_unions_join_epic_march_in_downtown_manhattan.html.

10. "Obama Gives Blessing to Anti-Capitalist Wall Street Protests," Fox Nation, October 6, 2011, http://nation.foxnews.com/obama-jobs-bill/2011/10/06/obama-gives-blessing-anti-capitalist-wall-street-protests.

11. "Obama Says Wall Street Protests Show Widespread Frustration, Predicts 2012 Effects," Associated Press, NBC New York, October 6, 2011, http://www.nbcnewyork.com/news/http://www.nbcnewyork.com/news/local/Wall-Street-Protests-Obama-Occupy-Wall-Street-Unions-Jobs-Labor-131221814.html3.

12. Russell Berman and Alicia M. Cohn, "Democrat-Backed 'Occupy Wall Street' Protests Turn Violent," *Fox News*, October 5, 2011, http://nation.foxnews.com/wall-street-protests/2011/10/06/democrat-backed-occupy-wall-street-protests-turn-violent.

13. "Updated: Obama's New Executive Order = 'Dream Act,'" *The Blaze*, August 20, 2011, http://www.theblaze.com/stories/obama-orders-his-own-version-of-the-dream-act-video/.

14. *Wikipedia*, http://en.wikipedia.org/wiki/DREAM_Act.

15. "Obama Pushes Congress to Make Dream Act Priority in 2012," *Fox News*, February 23, 2012, http://latino.foxnews.com/latino/politics/2012/02/23/obama-pushes-congress-to-make-dream-act-priority-in-2012/.

16. Sharyl Attkisson, "ATF Fast and Furious: New documents show Attorney General Eric Holder was briefed in July 2010." CBS News, October 3, 2011, http://www.cbsnews.com/8301-31727_162-20115038-10391695.html.

17. Devin Dwyer, "Senate Democrat Seeks Investigation of Obama's No-Bid Contract for Smallpox Drug," ABC News, November 25, 2011, http://abcnews.go.com/blogs/politics/2011/11/senate-democrat-seeks-investigation-of-obamas-no-bid-contract-for-smallpox-drug/.

18. Jia Lynn Yang and Nina Easton, "Obama & Google (a love story)," CNN Money, October 26, 2009, http://money.cnn.com/2009/10/21/technology/obama_google.fortune/.

19. Dan Gainor, "Soros Funded Lefty Media Reach More Than 300 Million Every Month,"Media Research Center, May 25, 2011, http://nation.foxnews.com/george-soros/2011/05/25/soros-funded-lefty-media-reach-more-300-million-every-month.

20. Buzz Patterson, "Obama Connection," Human Events, September 9, 2010, http://www.humanevents.com/article.php?id=38917.

21. "What is Viacom?," Opentopia, http://encycl.opentopia.com/term/Viacom.

22. Buzz Patterson, "Obama Connection," Human Events, September 9, 2010, http://www.humanevents.com/article.php?id=38917.

23. Buzz Patterson "Obama Connection," Human Events, September 9, 2010, http://www.humanevents.com/article.php?id=38917.

24. "What is Viacom?," Opentopia, http://encycl.opentopia.com/term/Viacom.

25. Buzz Patterson, "Obama Connection," Human Events, September 9, 2010, http://www.humanevents.com/article.php?id=38917.

26. "George Soros Biography and Political Campaign Contributions," Campaign Money, http://www.campaignmoney.com/biography/george_soros.asp.

27. "Obama Pleads for Patience on Economic Recovery," Fox News, June 11, 2011, http://www.foxnews.com/politics/2011/06/11/obama-economic-recovery-is-going-to-take-time/.

28. "California Gov Signs Landmark Law to Teach Gay History," Fox News, July 14, 2011, http://www.foxnews.com/politics/2011/07/14/calif-gov-signs-landmark-law-to-teach-gay-history/.

29. J. Dyneley Prince, "Review: The Code of Hammurabi," *American Journal of Theology* Vol. 8, No. 3: 601–609, http://www.jstor.org/stable/3153895.

30. Gabriele Bartz and Eberhard König, *Louvre: Arts and Architecture* (Könemann, Köln, 2005), 57. The laws were based on scaled punishments, adjusting "an eye for an eye," depending on social status.

31. "Code of Hammurabi" http://www.commonlaw.com/Hammurabi.html.

32. Chris Barker, *Cultural Studies: Theory and Practice* (London: Sage), 436.

33. Peter Saunders, *Social Class and Stratification* (Routledge, 1990), http://books.google.com/books?id=FK-004p0J_EC.

34. "Willie Lynch Letter: The Making of a Slave," Final Call, May 22, 2009, http://www.finalcall.com/artman/publish/Perspectives_1/Willie_Lynch_letter_The_Making_of_a_Slave.shtml.

35. *American Historical Review*, Vol. 19, No. 2, 217–229, http://www.historians.org/info/aha_history/wadunning.htm.

36. James McPherson and James Hogue, *Ordeal by Fire: The Civil War and Reconstruction* (2010).

37. Brian Steel Wills, *A Battle from the Start: The Life of Nathan Bedford Forrest* (New York: HarperCollins Publishers, 1992), 336.

38. Stanley F. Horn, *Invisible Empire: The Story of the Ku Klux Klan, 1866–1871* (Montclair, New Jersey: Patterson Smith Publishing Corporation, 1939).

39. United State Senate, http://www.senate.gov/artandhistory/history/minute/Civil_Rights_Filibuster_Ended.htm.

40. Mary C. Curtis, "Robert Byrd's Klan History and the 150 Recruits He Brought with Him," June 29, 2010, http://www.politicsdaily.com/2010/06/29/robert-byrds-klan-history-and-the-150-recruits-he-brought-with/.

41. "Al Sharpton: Reclaim the Dream Rally," August 29, 2010, http://www.youtube.com/watch?v=JCF2NECXr6g.

42. "Glenn Beck: Restoring Honor Rally," August 29, 2010, http://www.youtube.com/watch?v=IMq1W9fDvtc&NR=1.

Additional Notes

For more on Mubarak being asked to step down, see Anthony Shadid's article, "Obama Suggests Mubarak Should Step Down Now," *New York Times*, February 2, 2011, at: http://www.ndtv.com/article/world/obama-suggests-mubarak-should-step-down-now-82967&cp.

For more on Obama signing the bill for Native Americans, see the article, "U.S. to Sign Declaration on Rights of Indigenous Peoples, Obama says," *Star Tribune*, December 16, 2010, at: http://www.startribune.com/politics/112037629.html/.

For more on California's governor signing the bill for gay history, see the article, "California Governor Signs Bill Requiring Schools to Teach Gay History," CNN, at: http://articles.cnn.com/2011-07-14/us/california.lgbt.education_1_california-governor-signs-bill-gay-history-state-textbooks?_s=PM:US.

Our Faith: Ignoring the Evidence

1. *Wikipedia*, http://en.wikipedia.org/wiki/Glossolalia.

2. http://www.quotationspage.com/search.php3?Search=fish&Author=&page=2/ChineseProverb.

3. Zeke Miller, "Don't Compare Me to the Almighty, Compare Me to the Alternative," Business Insider, September 25, 2011, http://articles.businessinsider.com/2011-09-25/politics/30201080_1_gop-debate-pool-report-president-barack-obama#ixzz1cywIMcMl.

4. Colby Hall, "National Day of Prayer Service Cancelled by Obama, Causes Stir," Mediaite.com, http://www.mediaite.com/online/national-day-of-prayer-service-cancelled-by-obama-causes-stir/.

5. Alexander Mooney, "President Obama Marks Ramadan," CNN, August 1, 2011, http://religion.blogs.cnn.com/2011/08/01/president-obama-marks-ramadan/.

6. Billy Hallowell, "Barton Calls Obama 'America's Most Biblically Hostile U.S. President,'" *The Blaze*, http://www.theblaze.com/stories/barton-calls-obama-americas-most-biblically-hostile-u-s-president/.

7. "Willie Lynch letter: The Making of a Slave," Final Call, May 22, 2009, http://www.finalcall.com/artman/publish/Perspectives_1/Willie_Lynch_letter_The_Making_of_a_Slave.shtml.

8. James McPherson and James Hogue, *Ordeal by Fire: The Civil War and Reconstruction* (2010).

9. Judy Hull Moore, *The History of Our United States*, third edition (1990), 271.